ARTISTS' Handmade HOUSES

TEXT BY

Michael Gotkin

PHOTOGRAPHY BY

Don Freeman

ABRAMS, NEW YORK

CONTENTS

Henry Chapman Mercer
Fonthill

DOYLESTOWN, PENNSYLVANIA

Ceramicist Henry Chapman Mercer (1856–1930) channeled his early passion for archaeology when he designed and built Fonthill, a home that was both a residence and a curiosity cabinet, filled with artifacts from his studies and decorated with his own tiles and ceramics. Mercer named the house after a spring located on his property in Bucks County, Pennsylvania, but his Fonthill might also be a reference to Fonthill Abbey, the legendary home of the eighteenth-century English aesthete, writer, and collector William Beckford, whose residence was also a repository for collections from his travels and scholarly inquiry. Both Fonthills were touchstones for later generations of artist-built houses. Mercer, however, denied any connection with Beckford's home, perhaps due to the infamy of the latter's lifestyle. Mercer's own life's work was in reviving the dying industries of the area, and in the process creating an entirely new artistic endeavor in the form of his home.

Childhood trips to Europe and training with art historian Charles Eliot Norton at Harvard University fostered an appreciation and curiosity about historical art and design in the young Henry Chapman Mercer. After college, Mercer's family expected him to practice law, but when he returned to his family home in Doylestown, Pennsylvania, Mercer became interested in the historical material culture of the surrounding area, which he felt was rapidly disappearing. Mercer became a founding member of the Bucks County Historical Society, studying the vestiges of early industries in the area, such as ironworking, carpentry, and ceramics. He took a series of trips to Europe, where he gathered artifacts in Greece, Turkey, and Egypt, among other places. He also published a small book in 1885 examining a single carved stone found locally and thought to have been created by the Native Americans of the Leni-Lenape tribe. The book established his credibility as an ethnologist, and subsequent fieldwork launched his career as a gentleman archaeologist. By 1891, he had secured a position with the University of Pennsylvania Museum, one of the most important institutions in the United States for the study of anthropology and material culture.

Mercer's fieldwork, both locally and abroad, yielded scholarly papers, yet he grew increasingly at odds with the bureaucratic realities of the museum, and a dispute in 1897 led to his dismissal. That same year, he mounted a show to validate his collection of early American

LEFT: Fonthill's unusual roofline reflects its creator's eccentric yet organic design process. Mercer carved individual clay models of each room (forty-four in total, not including the basement) and configured them into a pleasing interior layout, before building the structure itself, upon which he built the roof, much of which is concrete. Mercer incorporated a 1742 farmhouse that existed on the site into his plans for the house. Encased in concrete, the original facade of the farmhouse is still visible inside the two arches. The weather vane on the tower is a depiction of Lucy, the horse used to haul supplies to and from the construction site.

tools, titled *Tools of the Nation Maker*. Mercer explained in the catalog that the artifacts "give us fresh grasp upon the vitality of the American beginning. At first, illustrating an humble story, they unfold by degrees a wider meaning, until at last the heart is touched." His efforts were, however, rebuffed by the local historical society, and Mercer decided instead to try to revive one of the old industries that he had studied—ceramics.

When Mercer initially failed to market ceramic vessels, he hit upon the idea of tile manufacture and created the Moravian Pottery and Tile Works. His ceramic tiles were inspired by a variety of historical precedents, and to his clients they appeared both medieval and modern. Although part of an ancient craft, Mercer's tiles found new success with the building industry, as they added pedigree to fireplaces and foyers. The Tile Works was initially housed in a series of sooty kilns on the Mercer family estate, but in 1907 Mercer purchased some property nearby so he could build a tile factory and also his home. The home he created was of neither a distinct historical style nor of a traditional construction as might be expected of a historian and archaeologist. Rather, perhaps influenced by his work at the museum, Mercer chose to employ modern and experimental construction methods and materials to build a home as a neutral backdrop for displaying his collections.

Constructed between 1908 and 1912, Mercer's home was one of the very first residences to be built of ferroconcrete, or reinforced concrete, which has earned his home a place in the development of modern American architecture. The house was designed from the inside out, with purposeful disregard for a cohesive exterior: "It was to be used first and looked at afterwards," he said. Mercer said the house was designed "room by room, entirely from the interior, the exterior not being considered until all the rooms had been imagined and sketched, after which blocks of clay representing the rooms were piled on a table, set together, and modeled into a general outline. After a good many changes in the profile of tower, roofs, etc., a plaster-of-Paris model was made to scale and used till the building was completed." Mercer's unorthodox, ad hoc modeling of his house necessitated awkward adjustments to connect the disparate rooms—winding passageways and abrupt level changes—which are one of Fonthill's most magical features, imparting a sense of adventure and discovery to visitors.

The romantically disjointed exterior of the house was a mélange of historical styles culled from a lifetime of extensive travels abroad, what Mercer described as the "literary and artistic dreams, and memories of travel." One of his memorable earlier voyages included a trip down the Danube River in a houseboat of his own design. During the trip, he visited romantic castles of central Europe, which certainly influenced the eclectic architectural massing of Fonthill. The concrete that Mercer employed also made it possible for him to embed his own tiles and his collection of historical ceramics in the walls and ceilings of Fonthill. He saw the decorative potential of concrete as a background field for his tiles. Improvising from an ancient Roman construction technique that Mercer called "earth vaulting," he described the process: "You stand up a lot of posts—throw rails across them—then grass—then heaps of sand shaped with groined vaults, then lay on a lot of tiles upside down and throw on the concrete. When that hardens, pull away the props and you think you're in the Borgia room at the Vatican." It was like archaeology in reverse: Instead of digging in the ground, Mercer and his guests could look up at a ceiling covered with myriad half-buried ceramic tiles, arranged in patterns or in narrative sequence against the neutral background of the concrete. His innovative use of ferroconcrete resulted in a house that is both a form and a surface, a sculpture and a text.

Mercer deliberately left the concrete raw and unpainted, appreciating the vitality of residual marks of the casting process. Noting that "the building is alive until we kill it," Mercer chastised the typical architect who "is afraid of the marks of the mold, the welts and the boards which show that the walls were cast, the spring of the vault not perfectly true, and the richness of the texture, that like the rocks of the world, reveals creative work." For his interior finishes, Mercer simply burned tar paper inside the house, adding a layer of oily soot to impart the mellow tarnish of age. Light fixtures were bare bulbs and furnishings were modest, early American antiques that offset the richness of the ceramic tiles and historical artifacts amassed throughout the house.

Mercer treated the public rooms of his house as an informal museum and a showroom for his ceramic tiles. Prospective clients could see the full range of his tiles and examples of how to artfully display them in a home. Mercer continued to incorporate his latest tiles onto any available surface right up until his death in 1930. After his death, Fonthill became not only a museum of ceramics, as Mercer had arranged in his will, but also a monument to his inspiring life. Informed by his proficiency in archaeology and seeking to revive dying handicrafts, Mercer ended up creating something new that served a modern building industry. By employing an experimental construction material, and by devising an unorthodox method for designing his home, Mercer earned Fonthill a place in architectural history and demonstrated the potential for architectonic space to surprise and delight.

PRECEDING PAGE: Though medieval in character, Fonthill is one of the first buildings in America to be constructed of reinforced concrete, an easily molded and fire-resistant material.

OPPOSITE: One of seven bedrooms and nine "chambers," each of which is unique, the Dormer Room was Mercer's original bedroom. The dresser on the right was designed by Mercer for the room, and the pictures above it are from his extensive collection of prints, more than one thousand of which hang on the walls of Fonthill.

ABOVE LEFT: The Dormer Room is visible through the doorway of the study. The stackable bookshelves on the left were made from milk crates; the telephone is actually an intercom, or one of several "house phones."

ABOVE RIGHT: The Dormer Room is the only bedroom at Fonthill with a sink, a convenience Mercer most likely first enjoyed abroad. The backsplash is blue-and-white Dutch tiles set among tiles of Mercer's own design. To the left is the Dormer Bath; to the right is the study.

FOLLOWING PAGE, LEFT: The Yellow Room, one of Mercer's guest rooms, was so named for the bands of yellow tiles set into its borders, vaulted ceiling, and fireplace surround.

FOLLOWING PAGE, RIGHT: The Yellow Room fireplace is one of a kind, as are all of the fireplaces at Fonthill. The built-in closet and dresser on the left were designed by Mercer for the room.

OPPOSITE: Albert Rosenthal's portrait of Mercer, painted after his death, hangs in the saloon above the small desk. To the left and right, concrete bookshelves house a section of Mercer's vast library. The stairwell at upper left leads to the central hall.

BELOW LEFT: The illustrated tiles surrounding the fireplace in the West Room depict scenes from Charles Dickens's *The Pickwick Papers*. The Yellow Room is visible through the doorway on the left.

BELOW RIGHT: A large photograph of Elizabeth Lawrence, Mercer's aunt, hangs at the top of the stairwell to the left of a Chinese roof-tile display. Upon her death, Lawrence left her beloved nephew a considerable fortune, which enabled him to build his dream home.

FOLLOWING PAGE, LEFT: The study, a room in which Mercer spent a great deal of time, reflects its owner's many and varied interests. The ceramic pottery collection situated just below the ceiling is held in place by chicken wire and includes Nubian black-rim red ware, c. 3000–2000 BCE, as well as Swiss lake-dweller shards, c. 10,000–5,000 BCE.

FOLLOWING PAGE, RIGHT. TOP LEFT: This stair leads from the Garret to the Columbus Room. Translated from Latin, the text on the steps reads, "HAPPY IS HE WHO KNOWS THE CAUSES OF THINGS." TOP RIGHT: The bookshelves on the balcony level of the library are concrete. Above them, the decorative ribs of the vaulted ceiling meet in one corner. BOTTOM RIGHT: This charming built-in dresser, located in the West Room, is made of concrete with wooden drawers. BOTTOM LEFT: This stair leads from the West Room to the central hall, the West Bath, and the Map Room. The text on the steps, translated from Latin, reads, "MY WAY IS YOURS."

PRECEDING PAGE, LEFT: This built-in, tile-covered concrete desk is located in the West Room, one of Mercer's guest rooms.

PRECEDING PAGE, RIGHT: In this corner of the Yellow Room, another of Mercer's many guest rooms, he designed a built-in closet. The elegant curtains are reproductions of the originals.

LEFT: In the study, Mercer used this typewriter for correspondence, articles, and books. On display are examples from his stein collection, and, on the second shelf down, of his own pottery. The skull is a memento mori, a theme further explored in this eclectic room's many prints.

OPPOSITE: The largest room in the house, the saloon was used for entertaining family and friends. Supper was served at long tables in the center of the grand two-story room. Prints from Mercer's collection line the walls.

FOLLOWING PAGE, LEFT: Mercer based the tile pattern on this ornate fireplace surround, located in the Morning Room, on a sixteenth-century Italian textile design. In 1928 he created a shelf list entitled "Books Pertaining to the History of Tools and Implements in the Library of Henry Mercer" and numbered the corresponding bookshelves. Number 33, made of concrete, is shown here.

FOLLOWING PAGE, RIGHT: The illustrations in the elaborate tile-encrusted ceiling of the Columbus Room were based on sixteenth- and seventeenth-century woodcuts depicting the arrival of Spanish explorers in the New World.

Paolo Soleri

Cosanti

Visitors to the Cosanti Foundation, architect Paolo Soleri's labyrinthine home, office, and workshop in the Arizona desert, are for the most part unaware that Soleri himself resides in a modest wood-frame house, obscured from view, in the middle of the compound. Cosanti is perhaps best known for the bronze windbells, based on forms and techniques pioneered by Soleri, that are manufactured, displayed, and sold on-site. Though visitors are free to explore the complex, Soleri is himself a private man, a study in contrasts that only adds to his allure.

The house in which he lives is one of only two structures on the property not designed by Soleri—the other is an Airstream trailer where his sister lives, next door to his own home. Soleri designed and built other structures that he intended to inhabit, but never did in the end. He was destined not to reside in the Earth House, an experimental, subterranean home that he originally designed in 1956 for himself, his wife, and young daughter; his good friends live there now instead. Soleri ascribes this largely to fate—the birth of a second daughter caused him to reconsider the size of the home—but it is also emblematic of his focus on community. Soleri, unlike many other artist-builders, is not interested in constructing a monument to himself, but rather in creating a sustainable social structure. Cosanti challenges the perception of the home as a disconnected refuge from the outside world, and instead weaves home and community together into an interconnected landscape that, more than fifty years later, is a rebuke to the high-end suburban sprawl of nearby Scottsdale, Arizona, which now surrounds it. Regarding the encroaching

sprawl, Soleri is dismayed by a society that is "suffering from a kind of flat gigantism that nails it to the surface of the Earth." His Cosanti is a complex and fantastical inhabited landscape—comprising offices, workshops, display areas, drafting rooms, residences, and gardens, interconnected on different levels by twisting paths, tunnels, and precipitous walkways—that recasts the home and workplace as an integrated environment.

Completing his architectural education at the Politecnico di Torino in war-ravaged Italy, Paolo Soleri (b. 1919) left his native city of Turin in 1946 for the United States, to study with Frank Lloyd Wright at his architecture school in Arizona—the Taliesin Fellowship. Initially detained at Ellis Island for more than a month, Soleri had ample time to sketch the Manhattan skyline. He described his first impression of Manhattan as "a beautiful landscape made of light." Arriving at Taliesin, Soleri was excited by the sense of community at the campus, but bristled under the dictatorial apprenticeship program. After a year and a half, Wright dismissed Soleri, perhaps angry that the Museum of Modern Art had published one of Soleri's designs for a bridge next to one by Wright himself. Heading into the nearby Paradise Valley, Soleri and his friend Mark Mills (also exiled from Taliesin) set up camp on the slope of Camelback Mountain. Surveying the desert from their hillside encampment, Soleri sketched designs for domelike homes in the desert, influenced by Wright's visionary designs and the surreal landforms and plants of the surrounding landscape.

Soleri's sketches came to life with his first commission to design a home in nearby Cave Creek, Arizona, in collaboration with Mills, who later established his own successful architectural practice designing experimental homes in Big Sur, California. The client, Leonora Woods, a Pittsburgh socialite, originally asked Taliesin Fellows to design her desert home, but, deterred by their high prices, she turned instead to the two outcasts. Her one requirement was a living room from which she could see the stars. Soleri created a subterranean home with a rotating glass-domed roof that, like a giant eye to the sky, could open, close, and rotate an opaque side in response to the sun. Respecting his client's modest budget, Soleri used recycled and low-cost materials, including military aviation salvage for the

OPPOSITE: The concrete roof of the North Studio was cast directly onto the carved desert surface, which was dug out afterward to create the space. This studio, which has served multiple purposes since its construction in 1961, is currently used to display ceramic and bronze windbells.

FOLLOWING PAGE: The North Apse was cast in place on an earth form. Plastic-sheet cutouts were placed over carefully smoothed sections of the form to achieve lighter-colored areas that contrast with the earth tones of the rest. Designs carved into the dampened form show as relief when cast.

dome and stones gathered on-site for the walls. In this, his first home, Soleri tackled issues of climate, sustainability, and landscape, which would continue to occupy his experiments in domestic architecture for the rest of his life. Photos of the Dome House, as it came to be called, were published to great acclaim in *Architectural Forum* magazine and were featured in the Museum of Modern Art's traveling exhibition USA Builds. The interior featured Native American–inspired patterns painted on a spiraling floor, similar to the one Soleri had been working on for the Guggenheim Museum at the time of his dismissal from Taliesin.

While building the Dome House, Soleri met his client's daughter, Colly. The two fell in love, married, and left for Italy in 1950 to meet Soleri's family. After the birth of his first child in Italy, Soleri improvised a mobile home for the family to travel in as they explored the Amalfi coast. The vehicle's design was influenced by Buckminster Fuller's Dymaxion car, as well as American Airstream trailers, and sported homemade sustainable features, such as a solar-heated water tank on the roof. In the fishing village of Vietri sul Mare, Soleri and his wife learned the ceramicist's craft from local artisans. In 1952, Soleri was approached by Vincenzo Solimene, an entrepreneurial ceramicist, to design a factory. The unusual project called for production, commercial, and residential spaces in one structure—a concept that would influence the subsequent design of his own home and workshop in Arizona.

In the wake of severe flooding in Italy in 1954, Soleri and his family moved back to the United States, with an idea of creating a sustainable lifestyle for themselves in the American desert. On a sojourn in Santa Fe, New Mexico, Soleri discovered a shop that produced and sold unique ceramic windbells. The Korean craftsman who made the bells had just died, and when the proprietor learned that Soleri had training in ceramics, he asked Soleri to take over production. Soleri returned to Arizona with his young family and purchased five acres, including a small frame house, in Paradise Valley, near Phoenix, where he produced ceramics to support his family and his innovative architectural practice. In 1956, he borrowed the technique of ceramic silt-casting to build what would be called the Earth House. "In the beginning," he said, "liquid clay was used to prepare ceramic objects whose shapes would be carved into the soil. Changing from fractions of square feet to many square feet and from liquid clay to concrete was simply a form of extrapolation. That which had been a pot became a house." The construction method for his home was disarmingly simple: Soleri first carved forms into the local silt, then poured a structural network of reinforced cast concrete, and then excavated beneath it. He began with the roof and excavated the basementlike interior later—creating a house in reverse. Soleri noted that the home was not an "underground house," but rather nestled "into the ground," and open at two ends to patios. The home is adapted to the desert climate—the surrounding earth keeps the house cool by day, while retaining solar warmth and insulating the house during chilly nights.

Soleri and his family were about to move into the Earth House when his second child was born, and the family decided to remain in the original frame structure, where he still resides today. To Soleri, his own home was ancillary to his larger vision of designing plans for megastructures and whole cities, as well as building a working community on his property. He created a foundry for bell-making and a laboratory for architectural, planning, and educational activities that would officially be incorporated as the Cosanti Foundation in 1961. The colony he had first envisioned at Taliesin had come into being at Cosanti, as apprentice architects, artists, and artisans experimented with forms, structures, and ideas. Construction at Cosanti continued to evolve with a variety of experimental cast structures beyond the flat roof of the Earth House, including piling earth into mounds and then casting domed and vaulted forms. Soleri also established a bronze foundry at Cosanti where he designed and fabricated sculpture, decorative objects, and architectural hardware, including doorknobs and drawer pulls, as well as his signature bronze windbells.

In 1970, Soleri had begun construction of Arcosanti, a city in the Arizona desert sixty miles north of Cosanti. Forty years later, construction of the city continues. While Cosanti is nestled into the earth, Arcosanti rises above the desert, resembling a spaceship, or a modern-day Saint Peter's Basilica at the edge of a canyon. Arcosanti is Soleri's prototype community for his theory of "arcology"—a combination of architecture and ecology. Many of the underlying principles of arcology were first incorporated into the design of his home compound. Cosanti, and its related parts, reveal Soleri's theory of "evolutionary coherency," wherein complexity exists on even the most microscopic scale, which creates an encompassing structure in the natural world. Soleri believes that man must mirror these complex and interrelated structures in his own communities. Cosanti not only functions according to Soleri's idea of organic complexity, but the compound itself also resembles a living organism; the various structures call to mind the beauty of such organic shapes as dendritic forms, skeletons, sinew, and muscle. Exploring Cosanti, one feels like Pinocchio swallowed by the whale.

Soleri never crafted furniture for Cosanti, choosing instead to live with a variety of mismatched furnishings, including white molded-plastic chairs. In a perhaps apocryphal story, Soleri describes burning some wood furniture of his own design for warmth on a cold night. "I am a miser," Soleri said with a shrug. Perhaps the name "Cosanti" itself offers an explanation. A metaphysical play on words in Italian, as Soleri explained, "It is a combination of the words for 'object' and 'before,' and it means 'there are things more important than objects.' Let's call it antimaterialistic." As part of his philosophy of frugality, Soleri has long practiced allocating scarce resources in a finite world.

OPPOSITE: This skylight is located in the poured-in-place concrete Pumpkin Apse, a space that is used as a model shop. Part of a large Plexiglas model of Arcosanti is in the foreground.

BELOW: The North Apse, which functions as a general entryway to the Cosanti Foundation studios, leads into the ceramics studio shown here. The earth-cast kiln wall in the foreground protected passersby from the heat of the kiln that was once located behind it.

PRECEDING PAGE, LEFT: This window is part of the north-facing wall of the Earth House.

PRECEDING PAGE, RIGHT: A display of bronze windbells hangs from the Bell Tree.

LEFT: A precast concrete pool canopy shades the swimming pool in the summer but allows maximum sun penetration in the winter. This twenty-two-ton structure, supported by wooden telephone poles, was cast onto the desert surface then lifted by two cranes into its final position.

ABOVE: Paolo Soleri, standing at the entrance to the poured-in-place concrete South Apse.

BELOW LEFT: Examples of Soleri's bronze sculptures are displayed on a railroad tie step.

BELOW RIGHT: A 1960s bronze sculptural bell assembly, which doubles as a light fixture, is suspended from the keystone of the North Apse. The abstract female form on the left was carved into dampened sections of the earth form using the simplest of tools: a knife and steel trowel.

OPPOSITE: The ceramics studio is below a red skylight and adjoins Soleri's drafting studio and office, which are accessed through the wooden door on the right. The roofs of these concrete structures were cast directly onto the carved desert surface, and the earth below was later dug out and washed away to form the studio space below it.

ABOVE: In the south courtyard of the Earth House, the outside half of a double cantilever table—used for outside dining and as a general work space—cuts through the kitchen wall.

OPPOSITE: The poured-in-place roof of the Earth House was cast directly onto the carved desert surface. The kitchen skylight, just visible in the upper left, floods the house with light in winter; in summer, both trees and an insulated panel provide shade.

OPPOSITE: A ceramic-bell light fixture hangs above the double sink in the bathroom of the Earth House. The door on the right leads to the bathtub and shower, the wall of which is common to the back of the fireplace, providing radiant heat in the winter.

ABOVE LEFT: This central fireplace heats the 750-square-foot Earth House in the winter.

ABOVE RIGHT: This bedroom is one of two small sleeping spaces in the Earth House lit by skylight.

FOLLOWING PAGE, LEFT: Six small sleeping areas, located along the east side of Cat Cast (so named because the earth pile on which the concrete was cast was mounded with a Caterpillar tractor) are divided by tilt-up concrete panels, which were cast onto carved earth. The colors, painted onto the earth forms prior to casting, adhere to the surface of the panels.

FOLLOWING PAGE, RIGHT: The rough texture of the earth-formed ceiling in Cat Cast contrasts with the smooth, colored concrete floors. Winter deciduous trees planted in two tree wells, visible through the windows, shade the structure in summer and allow maximum light to penetrate the interior in winter.

RIGHT: A cantilevered railroad-tie stairway leads from the lower-level sleeping area and library space in Cat Cast up to the kitchen-dining area and sleeping quarters above. Two bronze sculptures by Soleri are displayed in the cast-in-place concrete niche above the bed.

Russel Wright

Manitoga & Dragon Rock

GARRISON, NEW YORK

Perched on a cliff in the Hudson River Valley, Dragon Rock is both a craggy cave and a light-filled glass pavilion. The purposeful contrasts built into industrial designer Russel Wright's home are a summation of his varied career as an innovator of American lifestyle and are a call for experimentation and individuality. As an industrial designer whose work was geared toward the commercial marketplace, designing his own home offered Wright the freedom to create without restraint. "Dragon Rock, the house in Garrison, must not be thought of as a prototype—it is an exaggerated demonstration of how individual a house can be," he said. "I have been pleased to overhear some visitors to the new house say that they wouldn't live in the house even if they were paid to do so."

Raised in Ohio, Russel Wright (1904–1976) studied sculpture at the Art Students League in New York City prior to attending college at Princeton. His background in sculpture would direct his subsequent careers in both theater and industrial design. Wright first became involved in theater while at Princeton, working on weekends as an apprentice for Norman Bel Geddes, a theater designer who would himself later become a celebrated industrial designer. In the summer of 1927, while designing sets for the Maverick Festival, the annual arts pageant at the Maverick art colony, Wright met Mary Small Einstein, who was studying with the sculptor Alexander Archipenko at his Woodstock art school. Mary, who came from a family of prosperous textile manufacturers, married Wright the same year and helped him transition from designing props for the theater to designing decorative objects for retail. Wright's first household decorative objects were small metal sculptures of circus animals, based on those he had created for the Maverick Festival.

Wright began experimenting with functional objects in 1930, producing a successful line of bar accessories in spun aluminum. He liked spun aluminum in part because the metal could be finished to resemble pewter, a material often used in early American tableware. Throughout his career, Wright would be influenced by the historical foundations of the American home. His tableware stressed informal entertaining in a post-Depression household where the host and hostess rather than servants prepared and served a meal. He also pioneered what would later become ubiquitous: oven-to-tableware, pieces that came out of the oven and went directly to the table where they doubled as serving dishes. In ads he and Mary devised to promote his work, Wright stressed informality as a uniquely modern American attribute. Like many American designers of that time, Wright tried to define a casual indigenous American aesthetic, distinct from perceptions of both Old World formality and the severe Bauhaus design associated with Europe.

In 1939, Wright debuted American Modern Dinnerware, ceramic tableware that became his greatest commercial triumph and remains today the product most associated with his name. The ceramics line featured free-form organic pieces that were sculptural but had the heft of classic American tableware. In continuous production for the next twenty years, American Modern was the most successful mass-produced tableware ever sold. Wright added glassware, flatware, and table linens to the line, and also experimented with durable plastic tableware as an alternative to ceramic.

After Mary's death in 1952 and the uneven success of his newer product designs, Wright shifted his focus to his country retreat, which he had purchased in 1941 in Garrison, New York, and was situated on eighty acres of wooded hillside. Following a trip to Asia in 1955, Wright became inspired by the Japanese mix of theatricality and naturalism in everyday life to design a house and a landscape for himself. He adopted the Japanese penchant for combining traditional craftsmanship with an enthusiasm for new materials and products. Influenced by the Japanese ability to improve upon nature by creating naturalistic yet highly contrived designs, Wright began to transform the landscape around his home, which he would eventually name Manitoga. He planted and cultivated indigenous trees through which pathways and stone stairs meandered. Most important, he diverted a stream into an abandoned quarry, creating a pool that would become a dramatic backdrop. The name Dragon Rock was coined by Wright's young daughter Annie, who likened the place where pool met stone to a dragon drinking from a pond.

PRECEDING PAGE: Stone steps lead from the southeast corner of the main house to Wright's studio above. Most of the stones used to sculpt the architectural structures and surrounding landscape came from the property.

OPPOSITE: Wright removed one leg from each of the Eames chairs in the dining area to make them more stable on the uneven stone floor.

Wright decided to collaborate on the house itself with architect David L. Leavitt, whose Japanese-inspired designs he had seen in a magazine. Wright was an active participant in the formulation of the design of the house, particularly the interiors, but also in sketching the elevations, siting the home directly into the rock face of the quarry, and insisting (against his architect's advice) on a sod roof with pendant vines. Construction began in 1957 and continued for the next four years. Of the house, Wright said: "[It] is intended as an experiment and demonstration that contemporary design can create from old and new materials a home highly individual, capable of the variety of moods that can be found in traditional homes, a home that can join the emotional, sentimental and aesthetic characteristics with the practicality and comfort that we have created in the twentieth century." The house was featured in trade journals and popular magazines, including a spread in *Life,* showing Wright, his family, and friends amidst traditional American antiques mixed with Wright's own work.

Drawing from his early experiences designing for the theater, Wright planned his home as a staged experience. The carefully manipulated landscape around Dragon Rock became both a scene to be viewed from the house, as well as a setting from which to view the home. Entry to the house was from above, with the dramatic view of the surrounding landscape revealed during a descent into the sunken living and dining area. The living room resembled an ancient amphitheater, with pillows strewn on seating built into exposed rocks facing the panorama of nature seen through large sliding-glass walls. Lighting effects for both interior and exterior features, engineered by master lighting designer Richard Kelly, could be controlled from a single panel. Formica door screens were flipped twice a year to reveal different colors for winter and summer, and curtains, slipcovers, and accessories were also changed with the seasons.

In an open letter to his construction crew, Wright described how he wanted the house to relate to its surrounds: "There will be occasional 'blends' to bring the outdoors gradually in; for instance, blends occur at the lower part of the living room with a flagstone terrace, which will continue from the outside to the inside," he wrote. "On the other hand, the geometric regularity of the design of the house would contrast with the amorphic character of the land formation and the highly textured irregularity of nature's growth." He experimented with combinations of natural and man-made materials, embedding wildflowers and leaves into plastic wall partitions and pressing hemlock needles into epoxy wall paint to create textured walls. Inventive, labor-saving devices included counterbalanced shelves that disappear into the ceiling and drawers on the kitchen island that open at both ends.

Wright improved the land around the home with a woodland garden and a network of trails leading to a variety of landscape experiences. Wright's involvement with land conservation in this area of the Hudson River Valley led to a new career near the end of his life, first as a consultant with the New York State park system, and then, in 1968, with the National Park Service in Washington, DC. Wright developed a pilot program for summer activities in the capital's parks that continues today, and was adopted by other city parks nationwide. "My whole new career and philosophy is to help educate people to get enjoyment from the parks," he said. Wright's experience with the Park Service influenced him to open his own grounds to the public, much as Frederick Church had done at Olana a century before. Wright considered Dragon Rock not only a home for his family, but also a lesson in innovative design. After considering a number of ideas, in 1975 Wright deeded his eighty-acre property, with the exception of his house, to the Nature Conservancy, naming the preserve Manitoga, an Algonquin word meaning "place of the Great Spirit." "It is my idea of sanctuary," Wright said. "My aim here is to get people into nature. Americans don't seem to care about it very much; we don't have the tradition of respect for our environment such as you see among the Japanese and the American Indian." Until his death in 1976, Wright remained the director of the nature preserve, creating programs and events, planning a nature study building, and outlining a trail guide.

ABOVE: The main house appears to be built into the landscape above Quarry
Pond, just visible at the bottom of this photograph.

ABOVE: Wright's studio is connected to the main house by a pergola, which is laced with Dutchman's-pipes.

BELOW: Many native plants were incorporated into the landscape surrounding Manitoga, which Wright designed himself. *Osmunda claytoniana* (interrupted fern) and *Dennstaedtia punctilobula* (hay-scented fern) grow along the edge of Quarry Pond.

OPPOSITE: Wright designed the spun aluminum tableware shown here. The reversible Formica doors on the living room cabinet below are red on one side—for fall and winter—and white on the other—for spring and summer.

BELOW: The green walls in the living room are covered in epoxy embedded with hemlock needles. The resulting textured surface blends into the exposed granite of the cliff face. Wright designed the chair at center.

OPPOSITE: A stone stair curves around the trunk of a cedar tree, found on the property, into the sunken dining area. More than one hundred years old, this trunk is the main support for the south-east corner of the house.

RIGHT: Combining natural materials with a synthetic one, Wright pressed Queen Anne's lace and viburnum between two layers of Plexiglas to create the unusual panel to the left of this chair, the frame of which he also designed.

FOLLOWING PAGE, LEFT: The entryway to the house was inspired by Japanese architecture. Wright sandwiched a phosphorus substance between the panels of glass in the screen to the right to give the space what he called "a moonlight glow." He later replaced this material with small white Christmas lights.

FOLLOWING PAGE, RIGHT: Manitoga has a total of eleven sublevels. The stairs at left, in the main entryway, lead down to the mezzanine, which is in the foreground. The dark stairwell on the right, below the stone wall, leads down to the kitchen.

ABOVE: Wright designed this cattail-brown American Modern teapot.

RIGHT: The kitchen window, which is almost at ground level, looks out onto the rocks leading up to the studio. Wright designed most of the ceramicware on display.

ABOVE LEFT: The interior of the studio is divided by a bookshelf designed by Wright.

ABOVE RIGHT: The studio bookshelf and the door (when fully open) separate Wright's workspace from his sleeping area and bathroom. The open door leads to the studio terrace.

OPPOSITE: The wooden box in this close-up view of Wright's studio bookshelf contains slides he took on one of his many trips to Japan.

Henry Varnum Poor
Crow House

NEW CITY, NEW YORK

About an hour north of Manhattan, Crow House, the home and studio of painter, ceramicist, craftsman, and architect Henry Varnum Poor, survives today in nearly pristine condition, continuing to embody the ideals of the artists, writers, and designers who comprised the South Mountain Road art colony in which it was built. Crow House was a salon for this American Bloomsbury group, among whom could be counted Kurt Weill and John Houseman. Aside from Crow House, Poor would design several other homes for his accomplished neighbors in the colony.

First known as a distinguished American painter, Poor also pursued illustration, sculpture, graphics, fabric design, furniture-making, and, most famously, ceramics. At Crow House, he was able to combine all of these interests to create a complete work of art and design. Almost entirely handmade and employing a wide variety of media, Crow House is unique among American artist-built homes for its successful marriage between the ideals of the Arts and Crafts movement and the distinct sensibilities of modernism. Large, modern plateglass windows were set into handmade ceramic-tile sills. Cubist and Fauvist forms were hand-painted on beams and adzed onto rough wood furniture; the striking contrast between the modern and the medieval at Crow House gave lasting vitality to Poor's remarkable creation.

Born in Chapman, Kansas, Henry Varnum Poor (1888–1970) attended Stanford University, where he studied art. After serving in World War I, he traveled to London, where he became a student of painter Walter Sickert and formed ties to the Slade School, where he would get his first taste of a true artists' community. Poor was greatly influenced by a Cézanne show he saw in London, and it inspired him to travel to Paris to see more of Cézanne's work and to study at the Académie Julian. Poor then returned to California to teach painting and fell in love with one of his students, Marion Dorn.

Soon after they were married, the young couple moved to New York City, but disillusioned by the expense of city living and perhaps missing the outdoor lifestyle of California, they purchased property in the Hudson River Valley on the advice of Mary Mowbray-Clarke, an important figure on the bohemian art scene. Inspired in part by the Arts and Crafts ideals of a previous generation, Poor resolved to build his own home.

Named for the crows that continually came to hover above the building site, Crow House's construction began in 1920, and almost every element of the home was fabricated using materials found on Poor's property. Poor quarried and laid his own stone, and felled blighted chestnut trees to adze his own beams. He would spend the next thirty-seven years creating the curious amalgam of modern and historical sensibilities, playfully combining concrete-block construction and the Dutch vernacular architecture of the Hudson River Valley with the steep gables of French farmhouses, which he had observed on his tour of duty during the war. Images of Crow House were published in art and design magazines in the 1920s, setting off a near craze for artist-made homes and inspiring other American artists, such as Poor's friend Wharton Esherick (see page 186), to create their own distinctive abodes.

The day-to-day demands and challenges of crafting a house likely propelled both Poor and his wife to move away from painting and begin careers as designers in earnest. Practically every domestic accoutrement was conceived of and crafted by Poor, including framing timber, lighting fixtures, fabrics—even the front doorknob. He created his own ceramics from local clay and ground his own pigments for decorating his pottery, tiles, and textiles in his water-powered gristmill. Attracted by the idea of painting on objects that were also functional, Poor first experimented at Crow House with what would become his signature style of bold brushwork and Fauvist-inspired figurative forms applied to the surface of low-fired pottery. "I started doing pottery for the pleasure of decorating it, of having something in my control from beginning to end, so that both the object and the images it held would be equally mine," he said. Although Poor never abandoned his painting career and continued to paint murals for federal buildings in Washington, DC, ceramics would become his greatest legacy.

Tutored by neighboring textile designer Ruth Reeves, Poor and Dorn began experimenting with batik and other methods of painting on fabrics. Dorn started to win prizes and sell her fabric designs in Manhattan, yet, frustratingly, Poor never gave her credit for her contribution to the design and decoration of Crow House. With samples of her fabric in tow, she left for Paris and filed for divorce in 1923, embarking on her own illustrious career in carpet design—she would later become known as the "architect of rugs" in London.

Bessie Breuer, an editor at the *New York Herald Tribune* with ties to the French avant-garde, became Poor's second wife in 1925 and brought a new vitality to Crow House, introducing her friends Marcel Duchamp and Man Ray (who photographed Poor's house) to the intimate circle of residents at South Mountain Road. Breuer also raised the couple's two children and later became a novelist who fictionalized the sometimes-turbulent life of the art colony.

Poor expanded Crow House in the 1930s, adding a painting and pottery studio with living space above for his two children. The two floors were connected by a new spiral wood stairway, a feature likely inspired by a visit to Wharton Esherick's home in Pennsylvania, where such a staircase was used to dramatic effect. Poor also created a whimsical ceramic mural in the new bathroom that depicted a life-size nude woman in the shower. Custom bathrooms by Poor were soon in demand for Long Island mansions.

The newer rooms at Crow House were arranged in an arc, designed to track sunlight during the day. Different rooms in the house were carefully sited to capture maximum sun at different times of day—morning sun at the breakfast table and afternoon sun in the living room. Poor added other structures to Crow House, including a fairy-tale, half-timbered woodshop, a modern painting studio for himself, and a writing cabin for his wife.

Poor's versatility and lifelong involvement with pottery is still evident throughout Crow House—vases are set into niches and on tabletops, and ceramic plates rather than paintings are hung on or embedded into the walls. Decoration on his ceramics featured pictorial representations of family members, reinforcing themes of domesticity in his design production. As with his furniture, the display of ceramics was as much marketing as it was functional, and the handcrafted wares could be purchased by visitors to Crow House, along with custom architectural ceramic work on commission. In the pottery studio—along with the jumble of ceramic objects, shelves lined with pigment and glaze in glass jars, and notes and sketches still pinned to bulletin boards—one can still sense Poor's artistic energy and glimpse an authentic vestige of the vanished art colony of which Crow House had been the vital center.

PRECEDING PAGE: Poor built Crow House, here photographed from the rear, in three distinct sections, from local sandstone (quarried on his property) and cinderblocks. He constructed the oldest, central part with its steeply pitched roofs in 1920. In 1930–31 he added a second story over the painting studio; in the late 1940s he expanded yet again, adding a wing off the kitchen.

RIGHT: Poor embedded ceramic plates and tiles into the walls of his house and some of the outbuildings, a detail of which is shown here.

BELOW: From the house itself to its decorations and contents, Poor handcrafted almost everything— down to the doorknobs. This door opens onto the garden.

FOLLOWING PAGE, LEFT: Poor carved the kitchen sink, to the right of the window, from a massive piece of sandstone. The ceramic plates and shelf above are his, as are the wooden trestle table and cabinet.

FOLLOWING PAGE, RIGHT: Poor made the tiles for this stove, located in a corner of his bedroom on the second floor of the 1930–31 addition to the house. The ceramic vases on top of the stove, the painting above, the printed linen curtains in the window to the right, and the table and plates are also his.

PAGE 70: This small bedroom, where Poor slept in later life (and where, in 1970, he died) is on the second floor of the original wing.

PAGE 71: This sculpted clay head is part of a series of portrait busts that Poor made in the early 1950s.

LEFT: Ceramic pieces, including several portrait busts, line the large glass window in Poor's painting studio. A portrait of his lifetime friend and kindred spirit, Wharton Esherick, along with other paintings, lean against the wall; the chair at the old-fashioned desk to the right was made by Esherick.

BELOW: This section of Poor's painting studio includes a storage loft, accessed by a helical stair. One of the leading realist painters of his time, Poor taught and influenced many prominent artists of future generations. He cofounded and taught at the Skowhegan School of Painting and Sculpture in Maine; early alumni of this renowned artists' residency program include Alex Katz and Ellsworth Kelly.

BELOW: Poor built this fireplace in what he called his "new studio," an outbuilding he constructed on his property in the late 1950s. Above the opening, he painted a mural depicting Buck, the canine hero of Jack London's *The Call of the Wild*. On either side, he set his own hand-painted tiles.

RIGHT: This re-creation of Poor's new studio setup shows paintings from various stages of the artist's career. His tiered tea cart is visible at left. The two bottom, traylike shelves are filled with clear, poured plastic that is inlaid with wooden discs crosscut from a tree trunk.

OPPOSITE: Poor hewed the ceiling beams in his living room—the main room in the original wing of the house—from dead chestnut trees he found on his property. Likewise, he made the fireplace and arch between the living room and kitchen, which is just visible through the doorway, from sandstone quarried on his property. The ceramics and most of the furniture in this room are also his.

BELOW LEFT: The living room includes a dining area, which was a gathering place for many of Poor's artistic contemporaries. Here, Poor's trestle table—likely a gift to his first wife, Marian Dorn, and inscribed *July 17, 1921*, the date of their second wedding anniversary—is set for a small dinner party, a frequent occurrence in his day.

BELOW RIGHT: Poor created "portrait plates" of many family members and friends; the subject of this particular plate is unknown.

FOLLOWING PAGE, LEFT: As with most of the rooms in his house, Poor designed the pottery studio to take advantage of the natural light. His potter's kick wheel and its seat—from a Harley-Davidson motorcycle—are beneath the skylight in the corner. Plaster bats in various sizes are stowed in the shelves to the right. Poor's hand-painted architectural tiles are displayed on the floor.

FOLLOWING PAGE, RIGHT. TOP LEFT: One of the work surfaces in Poor's pottery studio. TOP RIGHT: This detail of a worktable in Poor's pottery studio shows both painted and ceramic portraits. BOTTOM RIGHT: A stack of Poor's hand-painted pottery. BOTTOM LEFT: Poor's hand-painted pottery and some of the sketches used in his book *A Book of Pottery: From Mud to Immortality*, which was published in 1958.

BELOW LEFT: The bathroom in Poor's new studio, built in the late 1950s, features his hand-painted tiles.

BELOW RIGHT: The 1928 bathroom in the original wing of the house was first displayed in the short-lived American Designers' Gallery in New York City, where it served as a prototype. The tiled shower features a hand-painted nude, just visible in the mirror above the faceted sink.

OPPOSITE: Poor's six-sided table, which he made in the early 1920s, is set in a light-filled corner of the new studio. Three of the table's sides are intentionally parallel to the three panes of glass in the bay window. The artist's sensitivity to the natural world is pronounced in the design and placement of this table and window, which overlook a stream through the woods on his property.

Raoul Hague

For more than forty years, artist Raoul Hague inhabited a primitive cabin in a valley in the Catskill Mountains, near Woodstock, New York, where he created his robust sculpted forms. Hague inherited an existing artist-built house and retained its historic integrity while modifying and embellishing the living quarters to make his own statement. Hague's rustic cabin is a personal space, evocative of a solitary artist devoted to his craft. The eccentric interiors of his home hold the notations, thoughts, and references for his large, abstract sculptures, which are housed nearby in modern galleries of his own design. In his sculptures, Hague studied fallen trees and worked methodically with hand tools to bring new life to the wood by revealing hidden geometries and implied human forms.

Inside his cabin, heated by a wood-burning stove and illuminated by glowing Christmas lights, Raoul Hague (1905–1993) was surrounded by the sounds of the forest mingled with the constant tick-tocking of antique clocks. Hague's guests have likened the experience of visiting him to being inside a Joseph Cornell box—a comparison that Hague reportedly resented. Although the two artists shared many of the same visual tropes, including collage, ballet, birds, mirrors, and clocks, Cornell's themes of enshrinement, memory, and yearning are quite different from Hague's work. Rather, Hague constructed his own cultural dialogue that he stapled, tacked, and nailed to the walls of his cabin. The tableaux that he created inside his home constitute a visual text that reflects his concerns with mortality and the endurance of art— how art and culture transcend time.

Hague was resolutely unsentimental about his life, home, and work, dismissing, for example, the importance of his extensive reading and its influence on his art. "Of course my reading could not influence my work—they are two different things," he said. "I am a person who uses his hands and eyes more than his mind. All you see in this room—the knick-knacks—I made them. I play around, yes. And for the last forty years I have been making large scrapbooks. Not about myself; I paste in them pictures and articles that have steered me." To contemporary critics, however, his home and its decoration, including the elaborate scrap-books that he compiled from his reading, contribute immeasurably to the interpretation of his distinctive work.

Hague, whose original name was Haig Heukelekian, was born in Constantinople in 1905. His Armenian heritage gave him a taste for fanciful embellishment, and his upbringing seemed to foster a desire for a contemplative and solitary life. As Hague said: "When I was five years old, my uncle one afternoon took me to a place like a store with a stove in the center. An old man was sitting there. He had a paper book and he was cutting the pages. His walls were lined with sewed, un-bound books. It was peaceful there. What a difference from the bedlam from our house, with six children, the mother and aunt and all. I have drifted to this old man's peaceful way of life in a cabin. I live in a cabin now. I chose this house because I saw his image here."

Arriving in the United States in 1921, Hague studied drawing at the Art Institute of Chicago, and changed his name to Raoul Hague for his vaudeville tango act. Dance and the human form in motion were to inform his later career in sculpture. Moving to New York a few years later, Hague studied sculpture at the Art Students League with William Zorach. In the city, he met fellow Armenian artist Arshile Gorky, who would have a tremendous impact on his work and on Abstract Expressionism in general. Hague also befriended painters Willem de Kooning and Bradley Walker Tomlin, whose insight he valued highly. Most important, Hague met sculptor John Flannagan, who took him on as a disciple, introducing him to the radical concept of direct carving—sculpting directly into stone without reference to a preconceived maquette. Flannagan also introduced Hague to the place that would later become his home—the Maverick Art Colony. Flannagan had sculpted the monumental Maverick horse from the trunk of a chestnut tree that marked the entrance to the colony. Hague periodically visited Maverick and occasionally donned a costume and danced with other artists and musicians in the annual Maverick Festival.

Working initially with bluestone quarried locally in the Catskills, Hague was increasingly drawn to wood, due to its abundance and what he called its inherent expressionist qualities. Hague named his sculptures after the location where he found the tree, or simply the tree species. Discarding the rough bark of the trees that he carved, Hague created large sculptures with richly finished surfaces that invite caress.

Hague befriended the Maverick colony's founder, author and printer Hervey White, who had also helped establish the nearby Byrdcliffe Art Colony with Ralph Radcliffe Whitehead in 1903. Maverick, unlike Byrdcliffe, was not a communal endeavor. Artists at Maverick designed and built their own homes, but were not expected to participate in community art production; the community at Maverick was a social, not economic, pact. White had built a small cabin for himself with bark-covered posts and beams in 1908 that also housed his printing press. This was the house that Hague would later make his own. His house, as well as the other artist-made homes at Maverick, was purposely small, more modest even than those of Byrdcliffe. White's frugal aesthetic dispensed with the affectation of handmade furniture, instead featuring a mismatched collection of store-bought chairs and tables—much of it in the Arts and Crafts style—as well as an attic sleeping gallery, a distinctive feature of his architectural work.

In 1943, toward the end of his life, White relinquished his home to his young friend Hague. The concrete floor of White's home, designed to support his printing press, would also bear the weight of Hague's massive sculptures. Hague designed his own storage buildings for his work, inspired by agrarian vernacular architecture seen on his drives in the region. A modernist take on the open-slat construction of corn cribs, the alternating slats of wood and Plexiglas protected his work and provided natural illumination for the on-site galleries.

Hague treated the studio walls as he did his scrapbooks, covering them with art, historical, and cultural references. He kept loose postcards in small boxes for impromptu decorating. Hague likened his collection of antique clocks to "temperamental teenagers," as they required constant attention. The clocks, frequently modified, were set to slightly different times, providing a continuous cacophony of chimes that Hague said kept him company and drove away unwanted guests. Hague also adapted furniture to suit his needs, customizing mobile book stands and pivoting reading devices. Though a voracious reader of art history, philosophy, and literature, he stored few books in the house, as he relied on lending libraries; a set of hand-bound encyclopedias was an exception. The cabin was illuminated primarily by daylight, and in the evening Hague enjoyed the low illumination provided by the colored Christmas lights installed throughout the house.

With burgeoning recognition in the art world, Hague's sculpture was acquired by major museums. But secure in his Catskills home and far removed from the New York art scene, he continued to refine his sculpture. He made regular trips to local libraries, and he occasionally entertained friends, including his neighbor, painter Philip Guston, and photographers Robert Frank, Rudy Burkhardt, and Lee Friedlander (who would photograph Hague, his work, and his home over the course of many years). Hague set up the Raoul Hague Foundation to care for his home and work after his death. After his death in 1993, one final sculpture stood—largely completed—in his studio, where it remains today, a testament to a solitary life dedicated to art and learning.

PRECEDING PAGE: A windowed dovecote, home to several toy birds, is a poetic threshold between the outside world and the interior of Hague's studio.

OPPOSITE: Above a window of his cabin, Hague installed two rows of mirrors, one of which remains for the enjoyment of the birds. From inside, he'd watch the sparrows come and go from the suet- and peanut-butter-smeared platforms he staged on the vertical metal rod below. Flanking the window are two lanterns made from inverted juice glasses and Christmas-tree lights.

BELOW: Hague's 1908 wood-frame cabin originally belonged to the author and printer Hervey White. The cobblestone chimney is typical of the architecture of the Catskills. The entryway at far left and the wooden, hexagonal bathroom at center, both designed by Hague, were added later.

RIGHT: The concrete floor in Hague's studio, originally designed to support White's heavy printing press, was equally well suited to the weight of the artist's enormous wooden sculptures. Amid carving tools and mementos, one of eighteen clocks modified by the artist stands on a shelf. A pastoral scene, framed in a toilet seat, is visible through the doorway on the left.

FOLLOWING PAGE, LEFT: Hague lit his home with red Christmas-tree lights, one of which hangs beneath a high shelf in the pantry.

FOLLOWING PAGE, RIGHT: Hague used the antique wood-burning stove in his kitchen both for cooking and for heat. The blackened stair leads to the cozy attic in which he slept.

ABOVE LEFT: Hague hung a small, motorized disco ball above his dining table. He would turn it on at night, and as it spun, it reflected the light from one of the many red Christmas-tree lights decorating the house in twinkling patterns across the ceiling and walls. To the left, a round, silver shade, fashioned from strips of silver tape, covers another Christmas-tree light.

ABOVE RIGHT: This clock with three hands is one of the modified clocks that simultaneously ticked in Hague's house. The outside ring of numbers denotes the days of the month; the inside numbers, the hours of the day. Behind the pendulum, the artist pasted an old dust jacket illustration—a romantic picture of a kneeling gentleman placing a shoe on the dainty foot of a lady.

OPPOSITE: Hague's daybed, which he used for napping, listening to music, and reading, is nestled in an alcove to the right of the dining table (not visible). A silver-tape light shade, as well as a clock, hang above. A stereo and books, including a set of encyclopedias that the artist bound himself, are set on the shelves to the right.

FOLLOWING PAGE, LEFT: Like pages in a scrapbook, Hague's studio walls are covered with postcards, clippings from magazines, and photographs that inspired him. He used the old compressor in the foreground to power his tools.

FOLLOWING PAGE, RIGHT: Though surrounded by figurative reference material, Hague never wanted to lose the "tree-ness" of the wood from which he carved his abstract sculptures. The piece shown here was the artist's last.

OPPOSITE AND BELOW: Hague stored his work on dollies in two rustic, clean-lined sheds that he designed himself and had constructed next to his cabin. Windows situated just beneath the ceiling illuminate the spaces.

LEFT: This tableau—a clock mechanism installed in a cabinet that Hague made, clamshell rosettes, a dictionary, and a photograph of the artist's relatives, among other items—evokes both mortality and the ability of art to transcend time.

OPPOSITE: In this re-creation of Hague's original attic sleeping gallery, a pivoting lectern of the artist's own design, complete with a light, is to the right of the bed. This simple yet innovative object is testament to Hague's persistent interest in the function and aesthetics of the things that surrounded him.

George Nakashima

NEW HOPE, PENNSYLVANIA

Though he originally trained as an architect, George Nakashima became so disappointed by the construction methods he observed being utilized in buildings that he changed course, deciding instead to start a career making furniture, which he could control entirely from design to construction and finishing. On this new path, Nakashima would become a great innovator in twentieth-century furniture design, with few rivals and countless imitators. Influenced by the craftsmanship and simple lines of traditional architecture in both the United States and Japan, Nakashima created a distinct hybrid of the two cultures in his hand-finished furniture and in the complex of buildings, including home and workshop, that he designed and built in rural Bucks County, Pennsylvania. These buildings combine his sophisticated understanding of architectural engineering with his respect for humble, vernacular structures. He produced designs that are modern yet imbued with the handmade quality and values of a bygone era, and they continue to inspire new generations.

Raised on the Olympic Peninsula in Washington state, George Nakashima (1905–1990) gained an early reverence for wood while hiking through the surrounding forests. He studied architecture first at the University of Washington and later at Massachusetts Institute of Technology. Upon graduation, Nakashima worked with several architectural firms in New York City, but when the Depression wiped out employment opportunities, Nakashima decided to travel, first spending a year in Paris. In 1934, he traveled to Japan to learn more about his heritage, and there he discovered a mentor in Czech-born architect Antonin Raymond. Raymond, himself inspired by the unique relationship the Japanese maintain between tradition and modernity, derived his first principles from the truth of the materials and the craft of fine workmanship. It was a commitment to fostering a deep appreciation

OPPOSITE: Nakashima designed the Arts Building, completed in 1967 and later renamed the Minguren Museum, as a tribute to his friend Ben Shahn. The southern facade, shown here, has a second-story porch and covered walkway to the cloister, a separate three-room building used to house guests.

for the time-honored rigor of crafting by hand while maintaining an openness to the demands of new forms that would later have significant resonance in Nakashima's own designs.

Returning to Tokyo in 1939, Nakashima became engaged to Marion Okajima, also originally from Washington, who had been teaching English in Japan. The couple returned to the United States, where Nakashima made a tour of recent architecture in California, and was dismayed by what he saw. "The architects were over-specialized and knew nothing about building," he recalled, "like cooks who draw pictures of cakes but can't make the batter themselves."

This experience was the catalyst that prompted Nakashima to begin to experiment with furniture-making, using tools he had brought back from Japan. Nakashima experienced a burgeoning spiritual sense with respect to furniture design. "Hours spent by the true craftsman in bringing out the grain, which has long been imprisoned in the trunk of the tree, is an act of creation in itself," he said. "He passes his hand over the satiny texture and finds God within. . . . It is this quality that is not to be found on the drafting board but in the experiences of the mechanic." His early experiments with furniture were published to acclaim in a California magazine in 1941, and Nakashima seemed to be on his way to a successful career in woodworking on the West Coast.

However, as the United States entered World War II, Nakashima, his wife, their infant daughter, and thousands of American citizens of Japanese ancestry were forcibly relocated to what were then called "evacuation camps." The experience had a profound effect on Nakashima and his work. The Nakashima family was interred at a camp in Idaho, where Nakashima befriended an elderly Japanese carpenter who taught him traditional Japanese woodworking. But when Nakashima's former employer, Antonin Raymond, moved to America, he offered Nakashima a way out of the camp by giving him a job on his farm in rural Pennsylvania.

After the war, Nakashima and his family remained in Pennsylvania, renting for a few years and then purchasing some hillside property near

OPPOSITE: Mira Nakashima's House, completed in 1970, has a reinforced concrete front porch from which the lily pond and gravel garden in front may be viewed.

FOLLOWING PAGE, LEFT. TOP LEFT: A stone picnic table is set outside of the Chair Department, completed in 1957. TOP RIGHT: An entrance bridge leads to the Conoid Studio (not visible), completed by Nakashima in 1960. The Chair Department, with its Conoid roof, can be seen in the background. BOTTOM RIGHT: This exterior view of the reception house (also called Sanso Villa), completed in 1975, was taken from the northeast. The windows of the tea room are visible on the right; a fieldstone chimney rises above. BOTTOM LEFT: The garden pool in front of the Arts Building.

FOLLOWING PAGE, RIGHT: Toward the end of his life, Ben Shahn created a cartoon for *The Poet's Beard*, an abstract mosaic fabricated after the artist's death and installed in 1972 on an exterior wall of the Arts Building.

the Raymond farm in 1951. Now committed to his profession as a woodworker, Nakashima chose to construct his woodshop before building the family home: "Like the farmer who first builds his barn, we built our workshop first." He and his family initially lived in a tent on the property while the home was being completed. Influenced by the rich examples of eighteenth-century American vernacular architecture in the area, as well as the masonry in neighboring historic barns, Nakashima worked with local wood and stone, his home anchored by a stone wall. "We built, quite literally, on the principle of laying stone upon stone," he said. "There is a sense of order and permanence."

Nakashima embraced construction as a kind of improvisation, noting that "the house was built without plans, and the detailing was developed from the material on hand or that which was available." The house was constructed without nails, and Nakashima employed prefabricated industrialized materials like corrugated concrete panels for the roof, which were purchased cheaply as army surplus. It is this unlikely marriage between American vernacular influences and Japanese sensibilities, along with a willingness to embrace the engineered forms of the modern age, that lends Nakashima's work its beauty and vitality. But Nakashima believed that it was the methods underlying design, and not (what he considered to be) superficial forms, that imparted integrity. "Perhaps the greatest drawback in domestic architecture is that only the forms change," he said, "but the methods are the same, whereas the greatest need today is a creative study of the 'method'—not merely the mulling of forms on paper or the building of models, but a synthesis of the techniques of building within our present requirements."

Most of the designs that Nakashima used in his home were replicated for sale at his shop. One of his most popular designs was a diminutive three-legged chair called "Mira" after his daughter, for whom it was first fashioned. Nakashima's furniture had clear lines of reference to early American furniture, such as traditional Windsor chairs, captain's chairs, and trestle tables, but Nakashima developed those basic style tenets further and produced his own unique models, creating, for example, a Windsor-derived chaise longue, or retrofitting the bases of trestle tables to chairs. Nakashima also admired the simple domestic interiors of the American Shaker community, and joked that he was a "Japanese Shaker," seeing the confluence of aesthetics between the two cultures. Over time, Nakashima became increasingly drawn to irregular shapes in wood, which he sought to preserve in his tabletops and chair arms; these irregularities became a hallmark of his work.

Just as he had been experimental with his furniture designs, Nakashima sought variety and contrast in the complex of buildings on his property. Only a few years after completing his home, he built a thin-shell, conoidal concrete studio with the help of famous engineers Paul Wedlinger and Mario Salvadori: The team created a soaring, arched ceiling that resembled a giant seashell. Nakashima also built a showroom and guesthouse, where visitors could view his furniture in a domestic environment. He added, over time, an expanded workshop, offices, an arts building, pool house, and a reception house to complete his compound. Maintaining Nakashima's home and business since his death, Mira Nakashima, who was trained in woodworking by her father, has developed her own line of furniture, some of it based on her father's original prototypes. Mira continues the evolution of design in which divisions between historical and modern are erased in the quest for structural integrity, innovative methods, and sculptural form.

ABOVE: This interior shot of the pool house, completed in 1960, shows the building's dramatic plywood barrel-vaulted roof. Nakashima's French Walnut Minguren III table and bench are sheltered below. The stools to the right of the table are Kikkoman soy sauce kegs from a Nakashima-designed Kikkoman display in New York.

RIGHT: The pool has an unusual cantilevered pool edge, also designed by Nakashima. The pool house is in the background.

LEFT: The woods are visible through the large door of the Pole Barn, a lumber storage building designed by Mira Nakashima's daughter, Maria, and built in 1990–95. Much of this lumber has been aging for years.

BELOW: Before chair assembly, hickory chair spindles are heated and shrunk in the bin in the corner of the Chair Department.

BELOW LEFT: This detail shows the corrugated transite edge of the cistern roof of Kevin Nakashima's House, completed in 1947.

BELOW RIGHT: Two Conoid Chairs are set in front of a Claro Walnut standing sculpture in the Conoid Studio. Sliding *fusuma* doors, painted by Mira in the 1960s, are on the right. Inspired by the shape of a seashell, the Conoid roof above, made of reinforced concrete, is only two and a half inches thick. The curves and tie beams are both structurally and aesthetically integral to its design.

OPPOSITE: A Conoid Room Divider, Conoid Cushion Chairs, and a Conoid Cross-legged End Table are in the foreground of this view of the Conoid Studio.

OPPOSITE: The living room area of the Reception House contains several Greenrock ottomans and a Buckeye burl coffee table. A Mira chair is visible in the background.

BELOW LEFT: This Odakyu Cabinet with *asa-no-ha* sliding doors, 1978, made of dove-tailed walnut, is in the Reception House.

BELOW RIGHT: The names of Nakashima's grandchildren and son Kevin are integrated into the tile work, which they designed, in the Japanese bath in the Reception House. The Nakashima family crest is on the wall to the right.

ABOVE LEFT: Cantilevered stairs, projecting from the wall, lead to the second-story loft of the Arts Building.

ABOVE RIGHT: The landing at the very top of the cantilevered stairs in the Arts Building is a raw concrete slab.

OPPOSITE: Bench backs double as a railing in the second-story loft of the Arts Building. Two grass-seated stools are set in front. Overhead is the building's dramatic hyperbolic paraboloid shell roof.

LEFT: An antique dough bowl is displayed on a small shelf against the far wall of the kitchen in Kevin's House. To the right of the bowl is a cupboard with sliding shoji doors.

OPPOSITE: The living room in Kevin's House has a Franklin-style fireplace. The furniture is placed on a rug designed by Nakashima in 1960.

LEFT: The narrow counter at right, with sliding wood screens above and a paneled storage area below, separates the kitchen from the dining area, which is hidden by the closed screen. A Conoid Chair is set in the corner, and part of a high Mira Chair is in the foreground.

OPPOSITE: In Kevin's House, a natural peeled post provides structural support and adds a decorative element in the door-way between the kitchen on the left and the dining and living areas on the right. Three Conoid chairs surround a Minguren table in the dining area.

OPPOSITE: Prints by Ben Shahn hang on the wall in the master bedroom of Kevin's House.

RIGHT: A wooden rocking horse, which Nakashima made for Kevin in 1957, stands in front of sliding doors in the hallway in Kevin's House.

Ralph Radcliffe Whitehead
& Jane Byrd McCall
White Pines
Byrdcliffe Art Colony

WOODSTOCK, NEW YORK

The empty halls and frayed burlap wall coverings at White Pines belie the fact that this house, a pioneering exercise in deliberately modest construction and furnishings, is still the heart of what is considered the longest continuously active art colony in America. Originally the home of the reform-minded couple Ralph Radcliffe Whitehead and his wife, Jane Byrd McCall, White Pines is the inspirational showpiece of Byrdcliffe, their communal center for art production and education set high on a hillside in New York's Catskill Mountains. The main house features ceramics, textiles, furniture, photographs, paintings, and metalwork in the Arts and Crafts mode, much of it produced at Byrdcliffe. Influenced by the theories of art critic John Ruskin and designer William Morris of England, Byrdcliffe was described by Whitehead as a "brotherhood of artists"—a community of artists, designers, and craftspeople dwelling and working together.

Ralph Radcliffe Whitehead (1854–1929) met his future wife, Jane Byrd McCall (1861–1955), in Europe. On an art-filled tour of Italy, the couple hatched their scheme to found an art colony. Whitehead had already traveled in Italy with Ruskin, his mentor from college at Oxford. Though Whitehead was born into a wealthy family of felt manufacturers from Yorkshire, England, he rebelled at the industrialization that had provided him with his vast inheritance and instead sought fulfillment in the Arts and Crafts movement. McCall, an aspiring artist from a socially prominent Philadelphia family, had spent much of her life abroad, also studying art with Ruskin, and later at the famed Académie Julian in Paris. Undoubtedly, the bonhomie of a life spent in the company of artists and writers would have predisposed her to the idea of community living in an art colony.

After marrying McCall in 1892, Whitehead published his philosophical manifesto *Grass of the Desert*, which outlined his ideas for an artists' community. Though the title referred to Walt Whitman, the content was based on the ideals of Morris. To familiarize himself with house construction, Whitehead apprenticed with master carpenters in Berlin and Paris before he and his wife moved to the United States. Settling in Montecito, California, they built Arcady, a Mediterranean-inspired dwelling overlooking the Pacific Ocean. They also built a Sloyd school on their property, a type of school that specialized in manual-arts education for children based on Swedish techniques. In 1902, Whitehead enlisted the help of two friends—artist Bolton Brown and progressive author Hervey White, the latter of whom would later found his own art colony—and they began searching for the ideal location for

RIGHT: This view of White Pines, as seen from the back, shows the servants' wing on the left. The stairwell leads to two maids' rooms and a cook's room; below is a pantry and other service rooms. The balcony on the top right is off of the pottery studio.

the projected arts and crafts community. After exploring areas of Virginia, North Carolina, and New York, the group settled on hillside farmland in the Catskill Mountains near Woodstock, New York. Proximity to the commercial center of New York City was a deciding factor, as the colony would need to manufacture and sell arts and crafts to support itself.

Whitehead found his true calling designing and building his own house and the extensive colony with his artist friends. The colony was named Byrdcliffe, derived from the couple's middle names. By spring 1903, enough buildings were constructed for the colony to open, attracting a diverse group of artists who built homes, designed wares, and taught. Early inhabitants included painters Birge Harrison, Carl Eric Lindin, and Herman Dudley Murphy, who would head the Byrdcliffe art school. Photographer Eva Watson-Schütze documented the Byrdcliffe colony, while painters Zulma Steele and Edna Walker became the chief designers of ornament for Byrdcliffe furniture and built their own home at the colony. The buildings of Byrdcliffe, in concert with Arts and Crafts ideals, featured locally felled timber (predominantly chestnut trees) with the unpainted wood left exposed. Stylistically, the buildings are an intriguing composite of influences from Whitehead's travels and observations. The Arts and Crafts architecture of California was clearly an influence, but also incorporated are traditional Swiss Alpine chalets designed for high-altitude living and rustic Adirondack lodges. Each of these styles was simplified to its essence and stripped of its decorative trappings and ornaments to create a unique rustic simplicity.

The same influences are present in the interior design of Byrdcliffe buildings. McCall endorsed "the principle of living like a peasant," albeit in a fifteen-room house. Indeed, the sparse interiors of White Pines stand in marked contrast to painter Frederick Church's grand home, Olana, located just on the other side of the Hudson River. White Pines was a stylistic and conceptual challenge to the perception of an artist's home as opulent and exotic, filled with the evidence of world travel. Instead, Ralph and Jane's artist-built home was intended to impart the values of a simple, modest lifestyle; as Jane noted: "A simple life is the best worth living."

In keeping with the simple-life concept, White Pines featured the extensive use of built-in furniture, including drawers, cabinets, and beds, which freed interior spaces for arrangements of chairs and occasional tables. A fireplace surrounded by glazed ceramic tiles (designed by Jane's cousin, Henry Chapman Mercer, at his Moravian Pottery and Tile Works in Doylestown, Pennsylvania; see page 9) is a rare ornamental feature in White Pines's sparse interiors. Ceramic vessels, many of them created by Jane at her on-site workshop and kiln, line the mantels and tabletops. Free-standing furniture designed communally at the Byrdcliffe workshops displayed simple joinery techniques and boxy outlines derived from British Arts and Crafts, but also perhaps inspired by the straightforward craftsmanship of early American furniture of the Hudson Valley. Decoration on Byrdcliffe furniture was derived from nature surrounding the colony.

Unfortunately, after only three years of unprofitable business, the furniture shop was forced to close in 1905. The Whiteheads instead became increasingly focused on their own ceramics production, White Pines Pottery. Other production facilities continued at Byrdcliffe, and an art school promoting painting outdoors flourished under a succession of directors. Artists continue to reside at Byrdcliffe to this day.

LEFT: Shown as it appears today, the Byrdcliffe Theatre was, in the Whiteheads' day, the Byrdcliffe School of Art. The wing on the left, now the box office and waiting area, originally housed Ralph Whitehead's library.

PRECEDING PAGE, LEFT: This Morris chair is in Jane McCall's bedroom. The door on the right leads to a sleeping porch. Jane made the painting and ceramic pots on display above the built-in chest of drawers.

PRECEDING PAGE, RIGHT: A pair of Chinese vases flank the base of the stairwell in White Pine's rustic main hallway. The lamp stand in the foreground was made at Byrdcliffe. The vase on the shelf above was made at White Pines.

OPPOSITE: Jane and Ralph used this section of their pottery studio, on the third floor of White Pines, to mix glazes. Everything in the space remains as it was when it was still in use.

ABOVE LEFT: Original unglazed pots, jugs, vases, and bowls are stored in the pottery studio.

ABOVE RIGHT: The bottom shelf of a closet in the pottery studio houses Persian and Chinese forms used to make White Pines pots, which were molded rather than thrown. Colored pots and wooden molds line the shelves above.

LEFT: The fireplace surround in the living room was executed by Jane's cousin, Henry Chapman Mercer (see page 9), at his Moravian Pottery Works; Ralph's initials, R.W., are worked into some of the tiles. The White Pines pots above and to the right were made by Jane and Ralph; the rocker on the left is an original Byrdcliffe chair. The doorway to the right leads to the main hallway on the first floor.

ABOVE: A hand-painted screen, executed after Ralph's death, depicts a map of Byrdcliffe. It stands in a corner of the downstairs dining room on the first floor of White Pines.

ABOVE LEFT: All the weavers of the colony worked together in the Loom Room, which was added to White Pines in 1906. A print of a madonna and child hangs on the white chimney in the back.

ABOVE RIGHT: The silks the Whiteheads would have used in their weavings are still stored in the Loom Room on a shelf.

OPPOSITE: On a shelf in the Loom Room, a classical Greek statue (not made at Byrdcliffe) stands to the right of a print of Botticelli's *Birth of Venus*.

ABOVE: The desk in Ralph's bedroom was made at Byrdcliffe. A turn-of-the-century Japanese print hangs above. A daybed made by Ralph is to the left.

LEFT: What is referred to as the "bridge" is actually a second-floor hallway connecting White Pines to the Loom Room addition. Peter Whitehead's fishing poles still hang above the windows.

OPPOSITE: Ralph's drafting table is positioned to the left of the door leading into his bathroom and, through that, into his son Peter's room. In the English style, the Whiteheads' sleeping quarters were linked: Jane's bedroom and bathroom connected to Ralph's, which were connected to Peter's.

Sam Maloof

Woodworker Sam Maloof built his home in the middle of a citrus grove, framed by the snowcapped San Gabriel Mountains of Southern California. This unlikely location called for clerestory windows and small-scale towers and turrets in order to capture the elusive light above the encircling lemon trees. These diminutive redwood towers, with peaked metal roofs painted Maloof's signature bright blue and capped by fanciful weather vanes, give the house the look of a toy town or miniature village. The entrance to the homestead is under an open framework bell tower, a modernist nod to the influence of California's historic mission architecture. Employing construction techniques of his own devising and furnished entirely with his own work, Maloof's handcrafted house grew room by room from the early 1950s through the 1960s as money and time allowed, ultimately forming a rambling compound enclosing a landscaped courtyard.

Considered to be a father of the American studio furniture movement along with Wharton Esherick (see page 186) and George Nakashima (see page 98), Sam Maloof (1916–2009) created a handcrafted home that is a testament to his lifetime work in elegant furniture design. Showing an aptitude for carpentry at a young age, Maloof designed cabinets for his family home while in high school. After serving in the army during World War II, Maloof went to work for Millard Sheets, a painter, designer, and the head of the art department at Scripps College in Claremont, California. There Maloof also met his future wife, Alfreda Ward, a painter and former director of the Indian School in Sante Fe, New Mexico. Ward introduced Maloof to Native American arts, and the two became avid and respected collectors, befriending Maria Montes and other important Native American artisans. Married in 1948 but lacking the funds to furnish their new home, Maloof turned to his carpentry skills and made improvised furniture from discarded shipping crates stockpiled at rail yards. Maloof was never comfortable in his role as an artist's assistant, so when his innovative furniture was published in a home magazine, Maloof was happy to begin his own career in woodworking. Industrial designer Henry Dreyfuss gave Maloof his first large commission: to furnish the Dreyfuss home.

Although his house was built exclusively with native California redwood, Maloof's furniture incorporated a diversity of exotic hardwoods that he warehoused on his property. The varying tones of the hardwoods were used to create pattern and contrast in his furniture. Maloof's early furniture was classic and clean-lined. Influenced by Scandinavian modern design, his work evolved into his signature curvaceous, attenuated forms that invite touch. His furniture is organic in construction, but also in the sense that it seems to be alive, inspired by the delicate anatomy of insects or the intricate dendriform of plants. Sam designed his

furniture from cursory sketches, then worked directly with a jigsaw, cutting each sinuously curved template to create the individual parts used in furniture-making. Sam and his team then fitted the joints and hand-finished each piece. These craftsmen, many of whom worked with Sam for decades, continue to create furniture using the guidelines originally established by Maloof.

Maloof's living spaces and workspaces are inextricably linked in the home, reflecting his idea of a connected, harmonious life. In the enchanted citrus grove where his family could reach out of a window and harvest fresh fruit, Maloof also began his furniture-making woodshop, which developed into a full-time business that continues today. The living spaces doubled as showrooms for potential clients. Living, working, sleeping, gardening, dining, and entertaining are distinct yet flexible spaces in Maloof's ingenious plan for the house. Doors from the woodshop open directly into the living areas of the house, and food from the kitchen can be brought to the shop workers, or served outdoors in a connecting garden courtyard under the shade of olive trees planted by Maloof. The whine of carpentry machinery is ever present, and Maloof worked daily at the workshop until his death at age ninety-three. Though his famous rocking chairs were always in demand, Maloof also introduced a few new furniture designs each year, and by the end of his life, he had made hundreds of variations on his distinctive cabinets, chairs, settees, tables, stools, and music stands.

PRECEDING PAGE: Maloof broke ground for his original house, built of native California redwood, in 1954, and continued to add to it, room by room, throughout the 1950s and 1960s. As he described the process in his autobiography, "I do not use drawings when I am adding on to the house. I just hold up a two-by-four and think, 'That looks pretty good,' and then nail it up. I do it all by eye."

OPPOSITE: Maloof crafted the dramatic redwood gates, through which visitors enter the Maloof Foundation courtyard, as he did most everything—by hand.

Rooms in Maloof's villagelike home are treated as distinct buildings, with individually articulated rooflines, and are connected to one another by short passageways or thresholds. Custom doors featuring Maloof's individually crafted wooden latches mark transitions between rooms, and entry into a room is celebrated by the pleasingly tactile experience of touching the organic-shaped latches. Highlighting transitional space, the brief encounter between two spaces is a key concept of Maloof's design aesthetic. Similarly, his furniture is noted for distinctive joinery, the structural component in carpentry that connects individual parts of furniture. Maloof celebrates what is customarily hidden in furniture construction. The structural joint, the connection between an armrest and its support or between a chair leg and a cross brace, is highlighted by Maloof's trademark pegs of deliberately contrasting woods.

In 1990, the Maloof home and woodshop were deemed eligible for the National Register of Historic Places, and the house began another transformative phase. When a long-planned California freeway extension project threatened to cut through the Maloof site, negotiations began to save the structures by moving them to a nearby location. In 2001, the state of California successfully moved the entire complex three miles from its original location. The original house was transformed into a museum, with all of its original furnishings and objects, while Maloof designed a new adjoining home for himself and his second wife, Beverly. The original house is now located on a hillside, and once-shaded rooms now have spectacular views. In order to provide the house with a remnant of its historical context, the original citrus trees have also been moved to the new site, reestablishing the grove around the house. Furniture-making continues at the workshop, and Maloof's artist-built home still provides an inspiring ideal for California living. The fragrant citrus plantings now also shelter the Sam and Alfreda Maloof Foundation for Arts and Crafts, which sponsors exhibitions for young craftspeople and fosters appreciation for crafts worldwide.

ABOVE LEFT: Sam Maloof, a master craftsman and a leader of the California modern arts movement, in his courtyard.

ABOVE RIGHT: Maloof's workshop, the building on the left, was moved to this location in 2000. The ends of fruit crates decorate its rustic facade. The building on the right, constructed on-site in 2000, provides office space and an additional workshop. The two structures are connected by a covered passageway.

OPPOSITE: Maloof's furniture templates are visible through the windows of his shop. Commissioned furniture pieces were made to order and sized according to the proportions of their purchasers. The necessary templates are labeled and stored in the event that a client wants more than one piece.

FOLLOWING PAGE, LEFT: Maloof made the pink-upolstered loveseat chair pulled up to the table as well as the other furniture in this informal sitting and dining area off the kitchen. He called the unmortared brick floors, which he used throughout the first floor, "singing floors," as they shift slightly underfoot. A portrait of Alfreda Maloof, Sam's first wife, hangs to the left of the white door.

FOLLOWING PAGE, RIGHT: This space, built in 1975–76, was originally Alfreda's two-story office and studio. By 1990 it was a gallery and showroom. The spiral stair, made from scrap wood, was added in 1997. Pieces from the Maloofs' collection of Native American pottery are displayed on the windowsill behind it. When viewed from the courtyard outside, the colorful stained glass window above the door reads "Alfreda."

ABOVE LEFT: Vessels by ceramic artist Robert Turner are displayed on the table of a Maloof dining set in the breakfast nook, off the kitchen. A pulley mechanism, devised by the woodworker, is used to lower the many houseplants above for watering.

ABOVE RIGHT: A close-up of the wooden cleats used in Maloof's pulley system for watering plants.

OPPOSITE: In this sitting area off of the kitchen, three paintings by Alfreda hang above furniture pieces made by Maloof in the 1970s and 1980s. The chairs are upholstered in fabric by textile designer Jack Lenor Larsen.

BELOW: The dining room, the first in a series of connected open spaces entered through the front door (at left), is dominated by Maloof's large, walnut drop-leaf dining table and benches. Used for entertaining, this elegant room, like all of the rooms in the house, is filled with artwork. Vessels by Kevin Nierman are set in the center of the table, beneath a commissioned chandelier by Carl Jennings. African tribal sculptures are displayed on the credenza to the right of the table.

OPPOSITE: The kitchen, which opens off the dining room, was designed and built by Maloof. It leads to the breakfast nook, the area in which houseplants are just visible at the very center of this photograph. Family pictures hang above the counters and cabinetry.

LEFT: The painting on display against the closet door in this first-floor sitting room is by Maloof's granddaughter, Amy Maloof. A wood-burning stove is set against a blue tiled wall to the left; a Maloof chair is in front. The stair to the right leads to a second-floor gallery space.

OPPOSITE: The bed in the light-filled master bedroom is set in the center of the space, below the skylight above. Maloof's swiveling lectern, for reading in bed, and the rocking chair are to the right. A sculpture by Albert Stewart is on the left, part of the Maloofs' extensive collection of works by significant Southern California artists.

FOLLOWING PAGE, LEFT: The ceiling beams in this rustic guest room are "supported" by lightly finished, found logs on stone bases, one of which is shown here. The pieces on the wall are by Susan Hertel, another prominent Southern California artist; a Maloof chair is to the right of the bed.

FOLLOWING PAGE, RIGHT: In this alternate view of the same guest room, which leads out to the courtyard, a photograph of Sam and Alfreda Maloof hangs on the wall. A Maloof swivel desk chair is in front.

OPPOSITE: Maloof designed and made many music stands, both single and double, one of which is shown here, in maple, in a second-floor alcove. Between it and a very early Maloof chair is a chest, one of a three-part set, for storing music. The bell tower in front of the house is visible through the window.

BELOW: Inside Sam's workshop, several chairs are works in progress. Templates and equipment line the back wall.

Frederic Edwin Church
Olana

Olana, set majestically on a hilltop above the Hudson River Valley in New York, is the grand-father of American artists' homes. Although by no means the earliest artist-built house in America, Frederic Edwin Church's home became the standard by which other artists' abodes were created at the end of the nineteenth century. Church chose a Moorish theme for his home, imbuing it with the mystery and exoticism of an ancient, non-Western civilization. Visible from miles around, and glowing fiery orange in reflected sunsets, Olana and its grounds resemble a scene from one of Church's vast, panoramic landscape paintings. A *tableau vivant* on a grand scale, Olana is more than just a house—it is a work of art. Designed by Church and tailored to his aesthetics, the interior furnishings reinforce the transformation of the commonplace into art, as domestic objects, including imported antiques, are sanctified through the touch and association of the artist.

Frederic Edwin Church (1826–1900) was the most successful American artist of his time. Born into wealth, then augmenting his fortune through sales of his large, radiant paintings of both domestic and foreign landscapes, Church decided to build a home that would reflect his world-encompassing view of art. He chose a farm on the Hudson River in New York, facing the western prospect of the Catskill Mountains, site of the Hudson River School of painting in the mid-nineteenth century. Cedar Grove, the home and studio of painter Thomas Cole (Church's mentor and a founder of the Hudson River School), was located on the opposite bank of the river and provided Church with a conceptual model for an artist's home in relation to landscape scenery. Cole's house was likewise oriented toward the west, offering a broad view of the Catskills, and was the subject of many of his famous paintings. Church actually boarded at Cedar Grove while studying with Cole from 1844 to 1846.

Church was also an avid student of the natural sciences, and in the 1850s he embarked on a painting expedition to South America in which he retraced German naturalist Alexander von Humboldt's route. The voyage resulted in Church's most famous painting, the mural-size *Heart of the Andes*, which is so detailed that viewers were encouraged to look at the vivid landscape panorama through binoculars. Church was also inspired by pilgrimage churches set high on mountainsides, an image he would re-create in some ways at Olana.

After marrying Isabel Carnes and buying the Hudson farm on which Olana would be built in 1860, Church began planning his home. He initially hired architect Richard Morris Hunt,

LEFT: The south facade of Olana, which includes the 1888 studio addition at left, overlooks the Hudson River and the Catskill Mountains. Decorative elements include polychromed brick designs, stenciled and gilded cornices, and patterned roof-slate work, all of which were designed by Church.

his neighbor in Manhattan on Tenth Street, where Church and some other famous New York City artists maintained studios. Hunt would go on to become one of America's most important architects, but after he had designed a cottage for Church and his young family, Church decided instead to collaborate with Calvert Vaux, an architect more attuned to his aesthetic vision of an integrated house and landscape. As cocreator of New York City's Central Park, Vaux was a logical choice to create a home that would be sited to take advantage of picturesque landscape views while at the same time serve as a contributing compositional element of those views. Vaux also had experience with the Moorish Gothic style that Church had come to love on his extended trip to the Middle East just before he began construction of his house in 1870. The project was a true collaboration, with Church drawing architectural plans alongside Vaux and devising schemes for the interiors and landscape. Church would continue to modify and expand his house on his own for the next thirty years.

For his interiors, Church borrowed the decor of a typical artist's studio and expanded it to the scale of a home. Studios like the one Church kept on Tenth Street displayed antiques and exotic objects used both for props in portrait sittings and as evidence of the artist's worldly minded sentiments. Church had accumulated art and antiques on his trips through Europe and the Middle East, buying Old Master paintings in Italy and shipping them back to Olana. He described the objects he chose for his home, saying "some of the other boxes have old clothes (Turkish), stones from a house in Damascus, Arab spears—beads from Jerusalem—stones from Petra and 10,000 other things."

When the house was completed in 1872, Church combined antiquities from different countries to create interior dioramas of scenography, evoking the mystery of foreign lands. He devised specific color schemes for the interiors, sometimes by filtering light from an outside window with colored paper sandwiched between two panes of glass. He also created much of the furniture in the house in conjunction with his friend Lockwood de Forest, a painter who would later create his own artist-built homes in New York City and then in Santa Barbara, California.

OPPOSITE: Through the arches of the bell tower, the "bend in the river"—where the Hudson widens to form Inbocht Bay—is visible. This "picture," as Church described the framed views from his house, is one of many spectacular views he contrived for the pleasure of visitors.

Suddenly revealed views, both in landscape and interiors, are key to Church's aesthetic, as in his famous painting *El Khasné, Petra*—the only finished studio painting that he retained for Olana. In the painting, the tomb at Petra is glimpsed through a narrow gorge, analogous to how rooms at Olana were laid out enfilade, room opening upon room, culminating with dramatic framed views of the landscape.

Church completely transformed the hillside landscape at Olana, planting hundreds of trees, digging a large scenic lake, and laying out miles of pathways and roads around the property. A succession of views revealed passages of scenery for visitors traveling by carriage. Modeled on European estates, his grounds were open to the public, and he strategically placed rustic wood benches as resting spots for those who chose to walk through the property. Olana and its landscaped grounds also painted a pretty picture for those traveling by boat on the Hudson River, particularly at sunset, when the honey-colored stone-and-brick home appeared to glow. Church's guests were afforded dramatic panoramic views of the river valley and distant Catskill Mountains from Olana's verandah. Large arched windows of different shapes and sizes offered views of the landscape, and some windows were even enhanced with decorative surrounds to convey the idea of a framed picture. On his trip through the Middle East, Church had seen homes in Beirut that he later imitated. "From the houses on the summit of the hill on which the city is built, the views are charming," he said. "The house tops are flat and generally have a room or two built upon them with stairs leading to the roof, so that it is convenient as well as agreeable to enjoy frequently the fine panoramas." The bell tower was the house's crowning feature and also provided guests with an ideal framed view of Church's spectacular grounds and the mountains beyond.

In 1888, though racked with arthritis, Church continued to modify Olana, designing and building a studio wing. "I can fancy the thought now passing your mind: 'Building a studio at his age with his infirmities!' Well, we will call it a mausoleum. It is solid enough to make a suitable shell for all the Pharaohs," he said. In his remaining years, Church focused his energies on completing his landscape designs for Olana and on personal sketch studies of the ever-changing views from his studio. Church had lived long enough to see his paintings become unfashionable, but Olana had become what it remains today—a monument to a great artist and designer.

PRECEDING PAGE, LEFT: This dramatic view of the Court Hall was taken from the main staircase, the design of which evolved through dozens of sketches. *Sleep*, the marble sculpture below, is by Church's lifelong friend, Erastus Dow Palmer. The peacock has long been a fixture in this elegant room.

PRECEDING PAGE, RIGHT. TOP LEFT: The room most associated with Church's eighteen-month trip to Europe and the Middle East, the Court Hall was inspired by rooms the artist saw in Damascus. The intricate stenciling in this room and throughout the house is original; designed by Church, it is based on designs found in books on Persian architecture. The execution of his designs was carried out by hired workmen. TOP RIGHT: Church's stenciled door, painted with metallic paint to reflect the light, opens into the studio from the corridor. The curio cabinet on the left, embellished with Indian carved teak, houses objects from South America. Church's *Christian on the Border of the Valley of the Shadow Death*, 1847, hangs above it. BOTTOM RIGHT: The fringed, lavishly upholstered chair at left, seen here in the sitting room, is popularly known as a "Turkish chair." Designed to evoke the exoticism of the Near East, this style of furniture came into fashion in the 1870s. The glass doorway on the right leads onto the piazza. BOTTOM LEFT: Church "framed" the landscape outside the decorative window, in the southeast corner of the sitting room, as he did many of the windows in his house, with colored and painted glass. The framed pictures are sketches from his travels.

ABOVE LEFT: *Spring*, 1857, is one of ten sculptures by Erastus Dow Palmer, an Albany-based sculptor, on view at Olana. It is displayed in the northwest corner of the Studio, to the left of a Chickering piano, on which diverse objects from around the world are arranged.

ABOVE RIGHT: Church's palettes and brushes are set on a table in the studio. The statue in the corner is a plaster rendition of Erastus Dow Palmer's *Faith* (also called *Supplication*), a wedding gift from Palmer to Isabel, Church's wife.

OPPOSITE: The sitting room is dominated by Church's dramatic *El Khasné, Petra*, 1874. A depiction of the most famous feature of the city of Petra, this painting was inspired by the artist's trip to the Middle East. Church designed both the frame around the piece and the fireplace below it.

RIGHT: Church added the corridor, from which this photograph was taken, and the studio, seen through the doorway, as part of a second building campaign. Charles Loring Elliott's portrait of Church on the left and of Church's father on the right flank the doorway.

FOLLOWING PAGE, LEFT: Church designed the elegant dining room, in which the family entertained lavishly, to double as a picture gallery for his collection of Old Master paintings. The large piece at far right is a depiction of St. Rose of Lima, attributed to the School of Murillo, c. seventeenth century.

FOLLOWING PAGE, RIGHT: Church's Old Master collection consists of several dozen European works from the sixteenth, seventeenth, eighteenth, and nineteenth centuries. The oldest work in the collection is an undated depiction of St. Peter, entitled *Anonymous Bearded Saint*, attributed to Pietro Perugino (c. 1450–1523). A small painting in a circular frame, it hangs at far right. The door is painted with one of Church's designs.

LEFT: The Church family's extensive collection of nineteenth-century china, glassware, and silver are on display in cabinets, probably designed by Church, in the Butler's Pantry, adjacent to the dining room.

OPPOSITE: Friends and family would meet in the comfortable sitting room to read aloud from Church's extensive library. The likes of Mark Twain participated in such gatherings. The open chest behind the Turkish chair (in the foreground) contains the Church children's egg collection.

ABOVE: The three paintings in this corner of the east parlor are by Church. The largest and most visible is *Autumn*, 1856. The rosewood drop-front desk in the corner is thought to be by George Ponsot. A large, painted Mexican bowl from the Uruapan region in Mexico is displayed on top, behind nineteenth-century Persian metalwork.

RIGHT: A portrait of Church's younger sister Charlotte Eliza, painted by George Baker, hangs in the east parlor. To the right is Church's *Twilight Among the Mountains (Catskill Creek)*, 1845. The rocking chair and settee to the right are nineteenth-century American; the tabouret table to the left is from Damascus.

Constantino & Ruth Nivola

At first glance, the weathered eighteenth-century shingle farmhouse on eastern Long Island might not appear to be an artist-built home. Though its exterior is modest, this home represents a radical experiment in living—synthesizing landscape, sculpture, architecture, painting, and historic preservation into a cohesive domestic and work environment. The first clue that this is an artist's home is the group of monumental sculpted concrete fruit on the lawn. These giant fruits were designed as children's climbing sculptures for a playground in New York City, one of Costantino Nivola's many public art commissions. These sculptures are also a witty nod to the vestigial apple orchard on the property. The sculpture marks the entry to the Nivola house, garden, and studio in the sleepy seaside hamlet of Amagansett, where Costantino and Ruth Nivola restored and transformed a derelict farmhouse into a place for living, art-making, entertaining, and experimenting with built forms.

Costantino Nivola (1911–1988), known as Tino, grew up in the picturesque hill town of Orani in Sardinia, where he, along with his father and brothers, apprenticed as masons. His wife, born Ruth Guggenheim (1917–2008), was originally from Munich, Germany, and her family spent vacations in Italy, and later moved to Turin. Tino met Ruth at the Istituto Superiore per le Industrie Artistiche, a Bauhaus-inspired art school in Monza, Italy. They married and moved to Milan, where Tino became art director for the design-conscious Olivetti Corporation. Fleeing Fascism, the couple relocated to Paris, where Ruth studied fashion design. In 1939, they settled in New York City, where Tino found work as art director of the fledgling magazine *Interiors*. The young couple befriended artists active in New York's burgeoning art scene at the time, including Franz Kline, Willem de Kooning, Jackson Pollock, and Saul Steinberg, an acquaintance from Tino's student days in Italy. Following their artist friends out for summers in eastern Long Island, the Nivolas purchased a dilapidated farmhouse that included thirty-five acres of farmland and woods near East Hampton in 1948.

Showing great respect for the vernacular architecture of the Long Island farmhouse, Nivola retained and restored the exterior, but completely transformed the interior that was originally divided into a series of small rooms. "I didn't know where to sit, in which room to sleep when I found myself the owner," he said. "Every wall had a door. I counted them. Thirty-five, plus five entrances. I felt like the Minotaur in the labyrinth." Nivola tore down all of the interior walls that were not load-bearing, stripping out the doors, moldings, and ornament, and roughly hand-plastered the ceilings—a bold, modernist move to create uninterrupted spaces, but one that also revealed a personal longing for the simple, hand-tooled interiors of his hometown of Orani. "The kind of remodeling I did was not dictated by any of the current trends in interior decorating or design, but rather by my own instinctive drive to come to sympathetic terms with the space, the furniture, and with the objects I need around me," he said. Nivola designed much of the furniture—simple low-slung seating and tables that provided a dignified and unassuming backdrop for the vibrant art and life of the household. Two murals command the interior, a housewarming gift painted on-site by French architect Le Corbusier. Staying with the Nivola family in Manhattan while working on plans for the United Nations headquarters, Le Corbusier was an early visitor to the reinvented farmhouse. Unexpected in a domestic context, the large murals anticipated or perhaps influenced Nivola's subsequent style of integrating architecture, sculpture, and painting in public art commissions.

The bright, open, and colorful interiors come as a surprise to visitors entering the historic wood-frame farmhouse for the first time. Bright yellow industrial paint, originally developed for tractors, covers the wood floors of the kitchen, the first room that visitors encounter. Nivola reoriented the main entrance from the front (rarely used by the Nivola family) to the back kitchen door. In a dramatic reversal of the norm for entertaining, guests were first ushered into the warm, intimate domestic space of the kitchen, and then served in the more formal living room, surrounded by Nivola's paintings and sculpture. Ruth collaborated on decorating the interiors, especially with regard to the textiles, patterns, and colors. Besides designing her own clothes, she also crocheted and

knitted throws and shawls. Once her two children were grown and out of the house, Ruth concentrated on her own art—jewelry and fiber art that she called "ornaments." Combining the handiwork that she had learned as a child with her experience in fashion design, Ruth knitted metallic thread to create intricate amulets inspired by forms observed in plants, insects, and marine life outside her Amagansett home.

The eastern Long Island location proved to be much more than a summer refuge for the Nivola family and would direct the future of Nivola's art. While building sandcastles with his children at the beach, Nivola experimented with pouring wet plaster over the castles. Inspired by the result, he later inverted the process by carving an image in the wet sand and pouring in plaster to create a positive relief. Replacing the plaster with concrete, Nivola invented a technique of sand-cast sculpture that synthesized his background as a mason in Sardinia with his art education, his experience with graphic design, and his burgeoning interest in architecture. One of Nivola's earliest commissions to employ this technique was the monumental wall relief sculpture for the Olivetti showroom in New York City in 1952. Fabricated on his property on Long Island, the precast concrete sculpture retained the rough texture of sand. The renown of the Olivetti showroom led to many major architectural commissions for the young artist.

PRECEDING PAGE: The back door, which opens into the kitchen, serves as the main entrance to the Nivola house. The small horse on the step is a model for eighteen cast concrete horses, which the artist created in the 1960s for a playground on New York's Upper West Side.

OPPOSITE ABOVE: Nivola created this mural and the one on the other side of this freestanding wall that he built behind his house. Using an Italian graffito technique, he drew by scratching into a surface of white stucco layered over black.

OPPOSITE BELOW: In his garden, Nivola constructed outdoor "rooms" suggested by freestanding architectural structures, such as the wisteria-covered pergola, fireplace, bench, and wall shown here. The artist and his daughter, Claire, would paint murals on this wall using water-soluble paint, which over the course of several years, would wash away. The two would then whitewash the surface and replace what had been there with something new.

Soon after completing interior renovations to the farmhouse, Nivola created an outdoor garden extension of his home in collaboration with his friend Bernard Rudofsky, an Austrian architect, curator, and author whom Nivola had met in Italy. Rudofsky, best remembered for the book and exhibition *Architecture Without Architects*, had long promoted the idea of outdoor rooms. Nivola, with his background as a mason in a Sardinian hillside town where people often built their own homes, must have represented something of an ideal to Rudofsky. Together, the men created an outdoor living area—a series of garden rooms loosely defined by freestanding walls, paths, hedgerows of vegetation, and pergolas. Shadows of leaves and branches enlivened and decorated the whitewashed masonry walls. Providing a tectonic foil to the wood-frame construction of the adjacent house, the masonry walls also retained heat, providing warmth and extending the use of the garden into colder seasons. An outdoor fireplace, brick benches, and a rough-cobbled floor recalling the streets of his native town became the center of the garden house, where Nivola cooked family meals, entertained guests, and worked. The outdoor living space, with sky for a ceiling, had the majesty of Pompeian ruins, but at the same time projected the dignified austerity of modernist design.

A laboratory, theater, and space for living, the garden continued to evolve as Nivola and his family added new elements, including plants, murals, fountains, and structures. What appears to be a giant, impenetrable cube in the garden was originally an outdoor solarium—four walls without roof or door, its interior accessible only by ladder—affording year-round sunbathing. Nivola also built a traditional Sardinian outdoor oven and a glass-walled studio to supplement the outdoor workspaces. Nivola's daughter, Claire, now an author and children's book illustrator, recalls how making art in the garden was a family endeavor, and how she learned by helping her father to cast relief panels, paint and repaint murals, and place objects in the garden. Learning the technique of wet-concrete carving, another of Nivola's sculptural innovations, Claire contributed sculptures of friends and family, pieces that stoically inhabit the garden and bear silent witness to the palpable sense of artistic experimentation at the Nivola family home.

LEFT: Over the course of many years, Claire created carved portraits of family and friends from cement-and-sand blocks prepared for her by her father. The figure on the left is a portrait of her mother, Ruth. In the foreground on the right is Nivola's carved cement-and-sand portrait of his grandson Adrian, Claire's nephew.

OPPOSITE: One of Claire's cement-
and-sand portraits stands in front
of the cement wall of Nivola's studio.
Nivola arranged many of Claire's
portraits in and around the garden.

RIGHT: A trumpet vine grows into
a sand-cast sculpture by Nivola.
Bas-relief depictions of his children's
plastic toys are visible on the surface
of the second row of blocks from the
top, and of Claire's hands along the
lower right-hand side.

BELOW: Sculptures from Nivola's Widows series stand on pedestals along the wall and windows of his studio. The work on the far left is bronze and the two pieces to the right of it are wood; on the far right, travertine marble sculptures flank a plaster model.

OPPOSITE: Nivola made plaster models, which he would bring to Forte dei Marmi, Italy, to be re-created in travertine marble. Artisans would chisel the pieces into shape, then the artist would finish them on-site. This marble sculpture is one example of the works that were completed in Italy.

LEFT: This bright sunroom over-looks the backyard. A terra-cotta water urn from Sardinia is to the left of the rocking chair. Old wooden toy hoops hang in the window. The wooden door leads to the cellar.

OPPOSITE: A sand casting made by Le Corbusier on Barnes Hole Beach in 1950 hangs to the left of the door between the living room and kitchen. Nivola used to say that he learned everything he knew about art from his Swiss friend, whom he taught to sand cast.

OPPOSITE: Nivola built the light in the corner of the living room from Tinkertoys and rolled paper. The painting above and to the left is by Paula Modersohn-Becher; the painted bas-relief to the right is by Henri Laurens. One of Nivola's series of Widows sits behind the plywood and polished linoleum table, which the artist also made.

ABOVE LEFT: Nivola was given the yellow tractor paint he used to coat the kitchen floor by the Mobil Oil Company, for whom he did a commission. When the sun hits this remarkable surface, the room is bathed in a honey glow. The coal stove, original to the house, was at one time a primary source of heat.

ABOVE RIGHT: Traditional handmade Sardinian baskets, in which women of the region carried things on their heads, hang in the back corner of the kitchen. An old wood stove is still used to heat this cozy sitting area.

BELOW: Le Corbusier created this mural, one of two he made for the Nivolas, in 1950.

BELOW: Around the corner from its companion piece, this Le Corbusier mural from 1950 shares a room with a wooden sculpture by Nivola, one of his series of Widows.

OPPOSITE: Nivola made this low bookshelf on which is displayed, from left to right: his early 1940s portrait of his wife Ruth when she was pregnant and three small bronze works from his series of Widows. Above is the artist's painted sand-cast sketch of the mural commissioned in the 1950s by the Italian typewriter manufacturer Olivetti for their showroom.

ABOVE LEFT: Ruth's bedroom overlooks the garden. Family photos and other keepsakes have been placed on and above an antique desk.

ABOVE RIGHT: Nivola's oil painting of Ruth hangs above the bed in this bedroom facing the street.

Wharton Esherick

Wharton Esherick's free-form shapes and smooth, flowing lines have been widely imitated since he began experimenting with wood carving in the 1920s at his eighteenth-century farmhouse in rural Chester County, Pennsylvania. Esherick, considered the grandfather of the American Studio Craft movement, originally studied to be a painter, but when he had little success in that medium, he turned to woodworking and ended up revolutionizing the field with his sculpted furniture and constructed environments. His design aesthetic was derived from modern art and, applied to woodworking, the forms he shaped pioneered a fresh approach to furniture design. Inspired by the craftsmanship of the local architecture, Esherick created his own home from the ground up on a high ridge overlooking the treetops of the hardwood specimens he would use in his sculpture, furniture, and architectural commissions. Esherick's career in wood began with woodcuts and picture frames, later evolving into chairs, cabinetry, and complete domestic environments that were essentially walk-in sculptures. In his home and studio, every room, every surface, every object and piece of furniture demonstrates the reinvention of woodcarving as a plastic art, unbounded by tradition. The irregular spaces of his home have the appearance of carved sculpture, but they are actually highly constructed works of engineering, as taut as the hull of a ship. Esherick reinterpreted the vernacular to create a home that was, both in its time and still today, utterly unique, handmade, and modern.

The son of a prosperous merchant family from Philadelphia, Wharton Esherick (1883–1970) rejected his father's desire for him to pursue a career in business, and instead studied painting at the Philadelphia School of Industrial Arts, winning a scholarship to the prestigious Pennsylvania Academy of Fine Arts in 1909. Frustrated by the rigidity of conservative academic training, he left the academy just before graduation. He sought a rural life where he could live simply while pursuing his Impressionist-style painting. In 1913, newly married, he purchased a small, dilapidated farm in Paoli, Pennsylvania, twenty-five miles west of Philadelphia. He used the old barn as his studio and gallery. His painting

career didn't take off as hoped, so in 1919 he accepted a job as an art teacher at the progressive, utopian community of Fairhope, Alabama, which would have a profound effect on his life. There he formed a friendship with the writer Sherwood Anderson, which led to Esherick's first experience working with wood. Anderson had been experimenting with wood carving at Fairhope because he understood the demand for woodblock illustrations in the publishing industry. He gave Esherick his first set of wood chisels, and Esherick went on to produce hundreds of woodblock prints throughout the next twenty years.

Returning to Pennsylvania in the early 1920s, Esherick needed to work harder than ever to sell his paintings, as he had borrowed money to buy the mountaintop overlooking his farm in order to prevent its destruction through mining or quarrying. In an effort to increase sales, Esherick carved decorative wooden frames and was surprised to find that his frames received more praise than his paintings. He also discovered that visitors were interested in purchasing the rudimentary wooden furniture he had crafted for his family's basic needs. In 1924 Esherick began to work with wood almost exclusively. His early furniture displayed low-relief surface carving as applied decoration, derived from his woodblock print techniques and perhaps influenced by the work of his good friend, artist Henry Varnum Poor (see page 64). However, while Poor shifted his concentration to ceramics, largely abandoning furniture design, Esherick continued to develop his experimental furniture, and the Fauvist- and Cubist-inspired forms became more than surface ornament and began to engulf the furniture entirely. Esherick created furniture as sculpted abstract forms, challenging the straight lines of traditional furniture design. Esherick recalled, "I was impatient with the contemporary furniture being made—straight lines, sharp edges and right angles—and I conceived free angles and free forms; making the edges of my tables flow so that they would be attractive to feel or caress."

In the early 1920s, Esherick and his wife, Letty, became involved with the neighboring Arts and Crafts community of Rose Valley, Pennsylvania, known for producing Gothic-inspired furniture. Letty, a dancer and

children's dance instructor, became involved with the community's fledgling Hedgerow Theater. Dance and the female form appear to have influenced Esherick's mature style. Approached by actors of the impoverished theater troupe, Esherick designed the seating for the theater, using a few hundred hammer handles that he had purchased at auction. With Esherick's direction, the actors finished the chairs themselves and upholstered the seats with painted canvas. The sculpted, yet functional, shape of the hammer handles clearly influenced Esherick's increasingly form-driven design. The unusual chairs were a hit with the local Philadelphia gentry, and Esherick began to obtain high-profile commissions to design furniture.

Esherick used primarily local hardwoods for his work, often harvesting trees from his own property, noting, "If I can't make something beautiful out of what I find in my backyard, I had better not make anything." Esherick claimed once that while burning wood one day, he saw a vision of a woman's figure in the fire. He snatched the charred log from the flames, and then and there began to carve the figure that he had seen. After this experience, he worked increasingly with whole tree trunks for both sculpture and furniture and quickly outgrew his old barn workshop. In 1926, he began to build a new studio that would later become his home. He chose a site at the crest of the mountaintop above his farmhouse, with a panoramic view of the valley below.

Esherick built his studio and home using oak and sandstone gathered from his own property. The surrounding area was full of farmsteads that dated to the original German and Swedish settlers in the early 1700s, whose traditional trades and craftsmanship Esherick admired. He

PRECEDING PAGE: Built in 1965, Esherick's elevated deck, here viewed from below, was the final addition to his handmade studio.

OPPOSITE, TOP: A stone path leads to Esherick's studio. The original structure consisted of the stone section to the left, which was built in 1926. A wooden addition was constructed in 1940, followed by a bath above in 1947. The cement block "silo," to the right of the front door, was added in 1965. BOTTOM RIGHT: Esherick built his 1928 expressionist log garage from local trees. The doorway is framed by a "ship's knee," or a tree trunk that had grown a horizontal branch. Esherick's 1930 glazed ceramic Winnie (Winnie-the-Pooh) stands guard. BOTTOM LEFT: A fanning stone stair leads from the studio entrance to the basement door below. The underside of the deck is just visible above left.

adapted local construction methods for his own home, including random stone work, board and batten siding, stucco-covered stone silos, and a feature especially unique to Chester County barns—stone rubble pillars. These stone rubble pillars were the inspiration for the towering, twisting rubble pillars that support Esherick's terrace. Similarly, for his garage, he borrowed log cabin techniques observed in Valley Forge, located near his home, but by using warped wood for its roof beams, he skewed its shape, turning a simple log cabin into a handcrafted, paraboloid form, a structure that would become popular in postwar modern design. Close examination of Esherick's furniture, especially his chairs, stools, and reading stands, also reveals a sophisticated grasp of engineering applied to the capabilities of wood. The curves in Esherick's furniture were determined by the flow of the wood grain; following the grain, rather than bending the wood, gives it inherent strength, as the natural grain structure remains intact. Esherick used root and limb wood, as well as trees bent by weather, to impart the twisting, yet resilient, forms to some of his furniture, such as his trademark dictionary stands.

Esherick was not opposed to using machinery to supplement his hand carving. "I use any damn machinery I can get hold of," he said. "I'll use my teeth if I have to. There's little of the hand, but the main thing is the heart and the head." Using traditional methods as well as his own improvised machinery to create modern engineered forms, including spiraling stairs, cantilevered decks, and twisting columns, Esherick imparted a sense of dynamic tension to his home, animating the remarkable spaces. Described by Esherick as his "autobiography in wood," his home contains the full range of his artistic career in wood, from small, free-form cutting boards to large pieces of furniture and architectural design. The home is a tour de force of the potential of the woodworker's art as ornament, form, structure, and environment. Esherick continued to work on and expand the house for the next forty years, until his death in 1970. One of the last architectural elements that he added was a three-level silo in 1966, where he layered varying tones of paint, one on top of the other, in a mottled, camouflage-like pattern. Upon Esherick's death, friends and family quickly rallied to preserve the home as a museum, and today it remains one of the most unusual handmade houses in the world, an utterly unique and pure expression of one man's vision.

OPPOSITE: Esherick's dining room overlooks the Great Chester Valley. His favorite seat in the house was the blue-painted bench in the corner, from which he could look out over the valley. His 1967 one-legged table was shaped to accommodate traffic passing through the door at right, which opens onto the deck.

RIGHT: Two of Esherick's handmade chairs stand to the left of the cherrywood kitchen counter, which curves at right. His swinging light and one-legged table are reflected in the asymmetric mirror.

BELOW: Esherick's 1927 expressionist carved cup rests on a cantilevered shelf that he fashioned in his kitchen.

OPPOSITE: This stair leads from the dining room to a bedroom above. Several of the artist's handmade sculptures are visible, including, from left to right: *No*, a 1934 bronze casting of a pearwood original; *Muse*, a Gabon black ebony piece from 1925; and *Her* (above), a bronze casting of a 1942 oak original.

FOLLOWING PAGE, LEFT: Esherick's 1966 silo kitchen features a cherrywood counter, copper sink, and fireplace for grilling. The window above the sink overlooks the deck; the artist called the western-facing window to the right of the fireplace his "sunset window."

FOLLOWING PAGE, RIGHT: Esherick's handmade salad utensils and martini mixers hang next to the sink in the kitchen. His handmade ceramic pots and carved cup are stored in the shelves to the left.

PAGE 196: The main gallery of Esherick's studio contains work from all stages of his life. Among the most noteworthy are his 1929 flat-top desk with its 1962 top in the center of the room; his 1927 Arts and Crafts–style drop-leaf desk, which stands against the far wall in the southwest corner of the room; and to the right of the drop-leaf desk is his 1928 *Pup*, which he carved for his young daughter Ruth. The sculptures and the woodcuts hanging on the wall are all his, as well as the chairs, the swinging lamps, and the music stand in the background.

PAGE 197: Esherick's handmade stools were among what he called his "bread-and-butter" pieces. To the right is a double music stand, originally conceived for two flutists who were husband and wife.

PRECEDING PAGE, LEFT: Esherick's small sculptures line the windows of the main gallery of his studio and sit on a built-in cabinet with an organically shaped top. Some of his many woodcuts hang on the wall to the left. A stool and chair are just visible below.

PRECEDING PAGE, RIGHT: Blurring the traditional distinctions between sculpture and furniture, Esherick's spiral library ladder, one of a series of library ladders, is a much-celebrated, seminal piece of American furniture.

OPPOSITE: Esherick's bedroom evokes a tree house. Accessed by a spiral stair constructed from the trunk of an oak, it feels tucked, like a nest, among the leaves and branches surrounding it. The unusual ceiling, with its rough-sawn rafters, suggests a woodland canopy, warped and uneven.

RIGHT: From his 1927 two-poster bed, set in a dormer, Esherick watched the moon rise over the trees. A sketch for his 1927 carved bust of Theodore Dreiser holds court from above; it looks down upon the artist's white easy chair, tusk-legged table, and a chair, which was designed for the 1939 New York World's Fair.

FOLLOWING PAGE, LEFT: Inspired by a photograph of Esherick's daughter Mary, an actress, gazing into a handheld mirror in her dressing room, his 1938 *Actress* sits on a table in an upstairs corner of the studio. Two stools stand below.

FOLLOWING PAGE, RIGHT: The central post of Esherick's 1930 spiral stair, leading from the main gallery to his bedroom, was made from the trunk of a large oak. The prismatic steps cantilever from the core. The result of this unlikely marriage of Cubism and rusticity is both functional and organic. This is one of Esherick's best-known creations.

Ruth & Robert Hatch

WELLFLEET, MASSACHUSETTS

The modernist, wooden summer cottage of artist Ruth Hatch is nestled into the dunes of a windy stretch of beachfront on Bound Brook Island, which is no longer an island but a neighborhood within the larger town of Wellfleet, a sparsely populated Cape Cod locale near Provincetown, Massachusetts. Constructed in 1960, the now extremely weathered house is an arresting sight in this wild, scrubby environment—the house itself has become like driftwood, although it still stands as a testament to its owner's ideals and its designer's ingenuity. The rustic, minimalist design was tailored to an artist whose work was entirely focused on the outdoors—her studio was the landscape that surrounds her home—but whose social life demanded ample space for entertaining. Though it was located in a remote spot, the Hatch house was expected to play host to lively parties.

By the 1950s, the Outer Cape had been a well-established summertime haven for artists for more than half a century. Ruth Hatch (1913–2007) studied with painter Edwin Dickinson, himself a link to the original artist colony founded in Provincetown by painter Charles Webster Hawthorne in 1888. Hatch's medium of choice was watercolor, and her near-abstract compositions were studies of the nuances of light on the layered Cape Cod landscapes of wind-pruned shrubs, lichen-covered rocks, scrub forest, and dune. Her art fostered a deep appreciation for the unique landscape of the Outer Cape. Summering in the area, initially in simple cabins, was a refreshingly rustic experience for the Hatch family, who spent the rest of the year in New York City. Ruth's husband, Robert Hatch, was executive editor of *The Nation,* and the Hatches were part of a New York circle of artists and intellectuals who were of like mind and made the Cape their summer destination.

It was on Bound Brook Island that Ruth and Robert Hatch met painter and architect Jack Hall, who had recently purchased a large area of land from writer John Dos Passos on which he would start an artist colony. Hall was a natural choice to build the Hatch cottage. Known affectionately as the "Squire of Bound Brook Island" for driving a Rolls-Royce on the dune roads, Hall was born into a wealthy family, was Princeton-educated, and had trained himself as an architect and industrial designer. As a painter, Hall created wonderful and mysterious invented histories—portraits of imaginary relatives from previous generations. Hall himself lived in an eighteenth-century wood-frame house, part of the original settlement in Wellfleet, and was familiar with traditional construction methods that could withstand coastal storms and floods. Free from the constraints of rigid architectural training, Hall became an innovative auteur, creating a series of homes for his family and friends, as well as industrial designs for the New York City firm of George Nelson and Company.

For Ruth Hatch, Hall created a home that appears to be little more than a skeleton of a house, stripped to its "bones" by exposure to wind and sea. In fact, the design itself accommodates little more than the bare essentials: Only the number of rooms required for summertime dwelling were included, although with hints of bourgeois amenities, such as an entry hall and a large living area for entertaining guests. The Hatch house was conceived as a series of cubes within a grid matrix on an eight-by-eight-foot module. Accommodating an unusual request from Hatch, the rooms were kept in separate enclosures and an outdoor corridor, open to the sky, joined them. Concerned about the exposed seaside location, Hall engineered an innovation to prolong the lifespan of the house: Huge wooden shutters, one per window and each hinged at the top, can completely enclose the house when it's not in use for the winter, or can be drawn up like enormous wings in summer to shelter the house from direct sunlight. Hall designed an unusual open deck that also reinforced the theme of the house as a framework.

Despite the clever attempts on Hall's part to protect the Hatch house from inclement coastal weather, the harsh climate, in the end, had its way. Author Mary McCarthy, who had been a friend and neighbor of the Hatches, describes a weather-worn cottage in her novel *A Charmed Life*, an acid satire about the midcentury intellectual summer scene in the Outer Cape. McCarthy depicts a fictional house on Bound Brook Island (called New Leeds in the novel) that is remarkably similar to the real one designed for the Hatches: "Beaten by storms, the house had weathered, so that it now seemed to belong to the landscape. The squat rectangular building, with futuristic hardware, painted gray originally and topped by a roped-off sundeck, now looked like an old-fashioned wooden icebox that had been wintering for generations on a New Leeds back porch."

In marked contrast to artists' homes of the same era that proclaimed freedom from architectural constraints through open-plan designs, Hatch maintained that the formal grid of the house actually allowed her greater freedom to arrange and rearrange the furnishings. Hatch decorated the interiors with furniture and objects from Design Research, the now-legendary modern furniture emporium, but took care to personalize the interrelated but discrete spaces with antiques, crafts, and thrift-store finds. Found objects, both natural and man-made, were also incorporated, as the Hatch family artfully adorned the home each summer with wildflowers, rocks, and fishing lures brought in from the beach. Interior fittings in the Hatch house were intended to be both utilitarian and beautiful—and, as always, a reference to the traditions and cultural touchstones of Ruth Hatch's beloved Cape: Lamp shades were fashioned from baskets, light pulls from nautical rope, and seating that doubles as a guest bed was upholstered in sailcloth. Interior walls of the cottage, textured and patterned over the years by salt-laden storm water, were used as a rotating gallery for the resident artists and their notable artist friends.

The Hatch cottage is now home to a second generation of artists. Ruth's daughter, Gilly Hatch, is a painter and lecturer at the National Gallery in London, and her husband, Tom Gretch, is an art historian on the faculty of the University College of London. Inspired by the artistic possibilities presented by the modern architectonic lines of the house and its rustic surroundings, Gilly's paintings capture the unusual geometries at the interface of architecture and nature, between the ordered and the organic—the quintessence of the sustained beauty of the Hatches' home on the Outer Cape.

PRECEDING PAGE: The hill behind the Hatches' Cape house, with its flat roof barely rising above the vegetation, is the perfect spot from which to view the ocean and check the tides.

FOLLOWING PAGE: This view from the north reveals the weathered deck and siding of the "master" sleeping house. The deck to the right overlooks the ocean.

BELOW LEFT: A deck separates and, at the same time, unifies the three structures that make up what the Hatches call the "Cape house": the main house to the left; the "master" sleeping house beyond (center); and the guest house, which is affectionately known as the "motel," to the right.

BELOW RIGHT: This photograph of the west facade of the house shows the kitchen shutter open.

LEFT: In the living room, a wood-burning stove, designed and built by a local potter, c. 1955, was used to heat the main house in the fall and for grilling meat during inclement weather. A painting by Gilly Hatch hangs to the left. A relief sculpture by Brading First is displayed on the top of the bookshelf.

FOLLOWING PAGE, LEFT: A painting done in the 1980s by Gilly Hatch hangs above the sofa in the living room's main seating area.

FOLLOWING PAGE, RIGHT: A watercolor by Ruth hangs to the left of the living room entrance. An oil painting, also by Ruth, is partly visible above the sofa.

LEFT: The end wall of the kitchen is primarily used for storage. Ripening fruit is set on a shelf beneath faded postcards and old labels.

OPPOSITE: Stones are gathered every summer and displayed on a shelf in the kitchen, next to a string of found fishing lures, accumulated over many years.

FOLLOWING PAGE, LEFT: The foyer of the main house includes a curtained-off storage area for coats, tools, and games. The collage above the chair is by the architect Serge Chermayeff.

FOLLOWING PAGE, RIGHT: This close-up of the shelf in the living room shows one corner of the painting by Gilly Hatch and, to the right, an early-twentieth-century religious icon depicting St. George and the Dragon.

BELOW LEFT: A collage by Marty Hall, wife of the painter and architect Jack Hall, hangs to the right of the doorway into the studio-study in the "master" sleeping house.

BELOW RIGHT: Robert built the plywood shelves in the "guest" sleeping house.

OPPOSITE: Postcards hang above a small shelf and a folding desk, both of which were made by Robert, in the studio-study. To the right of the pencil sharpener, a small oil sketch by Serge Chermayeff leans against the wall.

Michael Kahn & Leda Livant
Eliphante
CORNVILLE, ARIZONA

Near a river in the desert of Arizona's Verde Valley is the magical enclave of Eliphante, the sculpted environment that was home to painter Michael Kahn and his wife, weaver Leda Livant. The compound's name is a playful spelling of the animal whose likeness is conjured by a trunk-like entrance. Designed and built by the couple with help from their artist friends, Eliphante was their refuge, an attempt to completely merge the realms of domesticity and art-making. Kahn was known for painting mystical worlds on canvas. He then found a way to inhabit his art by extending his painted worlds into constructed space. Eliphante was constructed with both natural and man-made elements that were layered, collaged, and draped into a hallucinatory ensemble. Conventional domestic space is dematerialized into form, light, and color. Dizzying and labyrinthine, the domestic space of Eliphante is the manifestation of art as an all-encompassing endeavor.

Leda Livant (b. 1926) became spiritually possessed by Michael Kahn (1936–2007) and his art while on a family trip to Provincetown, Massachusetts, in 1970. Livant, forty-four years old at the time and a specialist in early childhood education, was comfortably ensconced with a husband and two children in Westport, Connecticut, and could not then have imagined that Kahn's art would carry her away from her family and home to a rustic life in a remote Arizona desert. Experiencing what is sometimes called Stendhal Syndrome (named after the French writer who described his art-induced collapse on a trip to Florence, Italy, in 1817), Livant all but swooned before a large abstract canvas by Kahn. Livant became suddenly aware of worlds beyond and the transformative power of art to evoke the intangible. Realizing that she had reached a turning point in her life, Livant left her family and joined Kahn in Cape Cod. There she helped Kahn realize his art and explored her own interests in drawing, painting, and especially weaving.

Kahn grew up in an industrious family who designed decorative metalwork for California outdoor living, including furnishings for hearths and patios. After attending the University of California at Santa Barbara and the Art Students League in New York, he moved to Provincetown in 1961 and studied painting with Henry Hensche at the Cape School of Art, where he learned to translate figurative subjects into compositions of color and light. After a sojourn in New York City studying figure painting and sculpture at the National Academy of Design, Kahn returned to Provincetown on a fellowship with the Fine Arts Work Center, where his aesthetic sensibilities were influenced by the distinct dunescape and ocean. He manipulated light in his paintings to conjure subconscious worlds beyond the canvas, undefined realms that suggest watery cataclysms, caverns, fire, and icebergs—some of the same imagery in J.M.W. Turner's light-infused paintings. Kahn's work from this period shares with Turner's generation an interest in the awe-inspiring potential of natural phenomena and its representation, as well as abstraction in art. In the late 1960s, Kahn's paintings began to change as the element of chance entered his work, allowing the process of painting itself to direct his compositions. Kahn's gradual artistic progression from landscape scenery to evocations of mystical worlds and finally to complete abstraction would later be chronicled in the sequentially staged installation art he created at Eliphante.

Life in Provincetown was relatively easy in summer, but Kahn and Livant desired a simpler life in a climate where they could devote themselves to art year-round and live off the land. They were attracted to the artist community around Sedona, Arizona, where they found a generous patron and employer in the rancher couple Bob and Jean Crozier, who permitted the couple to live rent-free and to build a house on three acres of their land while acting as caretakers. Just as the Atlantic Ocean had been a powerful presence in Kahn's art, so the high desert, an ocean of sorts, appealed to the uprooted couple.

Kahn and Livant began construction of their home and studio in 1979, proceeding, at Kahn's insistence, without a single plan or rendering. A firm believer in working contrary to conscious objectives, Kahn said, "Rather than intention, control, and seeking result, there was freedom, exploration and discovery, often with techniques and methods previously untried or purposely avoided." An earlier idyll in Crete had perhaps influenced the couple to create a subterranean home; their living quarters on the island had been the half-buried, overgrown ruins of a building bombed out during World War II. Their new home was built into the side of a hill, and the couple incorporated natural elements like rocks, as well as discarded construction debris, broken glass, and potsherds. Part of the flatbed truck that brought them west was incorporated into one of the structures, as well as seashells from Cape Cod—relics of the couple's past embedded into their future. A stream on the property provided water for the building site and also carried driftwood and other useful building materials to the site. Eight years in the making, the result is a magical, transformative artist's home, where the strong desert light is filtered through a multihued stained-glass ceiling and reflected across the brightly painted, circuitous interior by shards of broken mirror set into the walls.

Over the years, local artists, designers, and craftspeople befriended the couple and joined the ever-expanding construction project, contributing their expertise and collaborating on the improvised design. David O'Keefe, a landscape gardener and stonemason, assisted Kahn with the rock work and planning the grounds of the complex, while Michael Glastonbury, a British-born master carpenter and maker of fine musical instruments, created a kitchen for Livant. Glastonbury crafted wooden cabinets and countertops that appear to tumble in midair, inspired in part by the work of Provincetown artist Conrad Malicoat, who created fanciful brick tableaux for Cape Cod chimneys and walls. The kitchen provided a staging area for the couple's fine collection of handmade pottery, including works by Kahn and his first wife, Debbie, whose pottery had been their initial source of income in Provincetown. Livant's textiles were incorporated into the home as pillows, blankets, and throw rugs. Like Kahn's painted surfaces, Livant's hand-loomed textiles exhibit a broad palette, composed with a wide array of colored yarns.

Kahn's paintings were not hung on the walls, as the interior surfaces at Eliphante are themselves paintings—three-dimensional extensions of the themes and techniques of his canvases. Instead, Kahn devised a subterranean installation to display his paintings, where each canvas has its own sculpted, fabric-draped environment with filtered natural lighting. The labyrinthine gallery allowed visitors to experience Kahn's art as he originally intended. The caverns, tunnels, and eerie light create spaces that mirror those in his canvases. Kahn re-created the environment, recognized as a significant work of installation art, for his retrospective exhibition at the Northern Arizona University Art Museum in 1991. Unfortunately, the exhibition never officially opened to the public. Kahn had refused to comply with the fire marshal's demand to expose the illuminated exit signs, which Kahn had covered, as he felt they detracted from the viewers' experience.

Kahn's late works were paintings without borders, where the rectangular shape dictated by stretched canvas was merely an interruption of a continuum. "Forms were replaced by endless patterns," Kahn said, "as the multiplicity of randomness expressed an order." Both a landscape and a universe, Kahn's late paintings are one with the architecture of Eliphante, a collage of natural and man-made materials, where distinctions between walls, floors, ceilings, and furnishings are subsumed into a supernatural sculpted environment.

PRECEDING PAGE: Visitors to Pipe Dreams, an underground art gallery, exit through this whimsical hinged door made of wire, metal, and painted cement.

OPPOSITE, TOP LEFT: More than five years in the making, Eliphante is so named for its resemblance to an elephant. When viewed from above, the tunnel-like front entrance suggests the trunk, and the main room, just visible behind the tree branches, its head and eyes. TOP RIGHT: Leda Livant stands in front of *Homage to Gaudi*, a driftwood and stone work made by Kahn after the couples' trip to Barcelona in 2003. BOTTOM: Pipe Dreams, here viewed from the side, houses a permanent installation of Kahn's work. The AstroTurf in the foreground, donated by a local tennis club, keeps dust and weeds at bay.

FOLLOWING PAGE, LEFT: Kahn and Livant made the tunnel entrance to the main room in Eliphante from metal rods shaped into arches and covered with wire lath and cement, which they painted.

FOLLOWING PAGE, RIGHT: Kahn created the "stained-glass" windows in Eliphante by gluing pieces of colored glass onto sheets of found plate glass. The structural components in between the glass panels are painted cement over chicken wire.

RIGHT: Christmas lights, clustered in holes in the ceiling, provide additional light in Eliphante's multilevel main room, which is constructed almost entirely of scavenged and donated materials, including piled stones, driftwood, and concrete molded over chicken wire or metal rods.

LEFT: There are very few, if any, straight lines in Eliphante, as evidenced by the undulating, organic structure of the main room, which is essentially round. The dark hole to the left is the entrance tunnel; the bright area above is the sleeping loft.

ABOVE: One of a series of twelve paintings that Kahn did between 1970 and 1976, *Ancrambdale*, four-by-five feet, is housed in Pipe Dreams. The first canvas the artist rotated as he painted it, there is no top or bottom, and it may be hung from whichever edge one desires.

LEFT: Much of the painted eight-foot adobe wall in this view of Eliphante's spectacular main room is composed of dirt, water, dried leaves and weeds, and rammed earth. A mirrored construction is embedded in the section above the piano, which is surrounded by driftwood. To the right of the piano, cupboard doors made of carved scrap wood are slightly open. At far right, a small mosaic and pottery shards are stacked among the stones.

BELOW: Michael Glastonbury, whom Kahn considered a "true artistic brother," created the free-form kitchen counter in Hipodome—another building on the compound, as well as Kahn and Livant's one-time residence—from redwood and a bit of pine.

OPPOSITE: A wood stove on the other side of the kitchen space is used for heating and cooking. A sleeping loft and Mylar ceiling are above.

BELOW: Pottery shards are embedded in the wall above what was going to be the kitchen sink in Eliphante. Kahn and Livant originally planned to live in Eliphante, their handmade creation, but they eventually came to the conclusion that it should be enjoyed and experienced as an art space. Though well suited for temporary gatherings, it did not provide adequate, long-term shelter.

OPPOSITE: In the solar-heated bathhouse, the wall above the bathtub, which is visible at lower right, is painted rammed earth. The sink is in the nook to the right of the door, below the mirror and stained-glass window.

ABOVE LEFT: Kahn and Livant converted the ten-by-twelve-foot flatbed truck in which they traveled from Cape Cod to Arizona, into the guest room and studio shown here.

ABOVE RIGHT: The last chamber in Pipe Dreams, this room features a giant tassel by Elizabeth March, hung among pillows, draped fabric, and scrap rugs.

OPPOSITE: In Hipodome, where Kahn and Livant resided at one time, a couch draped in Livant's weavings is set against the painted rammed-earth wall in the living room area opposite the fireplace.

VISITOR INFORMATION

The following houses are open to the public.
Many have limited hours and require reservations, so when planning
your trip, check the websites and call ahead for details.

Fonthill Museum
East Court Street and Route 313
Doylestown, PA 18901
215.348.9462
www.mercermuseum.org

Olana
5720 State Route 9G
Hudson, NY 12534
518.828.0135
www.olana.org

George Nakashima
1847 Aquetong Road
New Hope, PA 18938
215.862.2272
www.nakashimawoodworker.com

The Russel Wright Design Center
584 Route 9D
Garrison, NY 10524
845.424.3812
www.russelwrightcenter.org

Sam and Alfreda Maloof Foundation for Arts and Crafts
5131 Carnelian Street
Alta Loma, CA 91701
909.980.0412
www.malooffoundation.org

Cosanti
6433 East Doubletree Ranch Road
Scottsdale, AZ 85253
480.948.6145
www.arcosanti.org

The Wharton Esherick Museum
610.644.5822
www.whartonesherickmuseum.org

Byrdcliffe Art Colony
34 Tinker Street
Woodstock, NY 12498
845.679.2079
www.woodstockguild.org

ACKNOWLEDGMENTS

Both the author and photographer would like to extend their gratitude to the following people who devoted their time and expertise to help realize this project: Cosanti Foundation—Paolo Soleri, Mary Hoadley, Roger Tomalty, Abel Alday, Alfonso Elia, Melanie Husband, Hannelore Kirsch, Michael Cahill, Linda Bonnette, Virginia Bateman; Sam and Alfreda Maloof Foundation for Arts and Crafts and Maloof Woodworking—Sam Maloof, Bevery Maloof, Roslyn Bok, Larry White, David Wade, Mike Johnson, Seth; George Nakashima Woodworker, S.A.—Mira Nakashima; Fonthill and Mercer Museums—Ed Reidell, Molly Lowell, Carol McMaugh; The Raoul Hague Foundation—Jill Weinberg Adams, Bill Mead; Woodstock Byrdcliffe Guild—Henry T. Ford, Carla T. Smith; Hatch Cottage—Gilly Hatch, Tom Gretton, Peter McMahon of the Cape Cod Modern House Trust, George Price and Bill Burke of the Cape Cod National Seashore, Noa Hall, Sandy Rose, Francis Biddle; Olana State Historic Site—Evelyn Trebilcock, Mark Prezorski; Crow House—Peter Poor, Anna Poor, Martus Granier, Cameron Shay, Priscilla Caldwell; Nivola House—Claire Nivola, Gus Kiley, Pietro Nivola, Kara Westerman; Eliphante Ltd.—Leda Livant, J.D. Allen of Blue Feather Tours; Manitoga and The Russel Wright Design Center—Lori Moss; The Wharton Esherick Museum—Robert Leonard.

I would like to thank Mi-khoo Nantawan Khoosuwan, Judy Rhee, and George Barberis for their generous and invaluable time and assistance. Also, Jayne Baum of JHB Gallery; Frank Parvis of i2i; and Rupert Thomas, the editor of *World of Interiors,* who commissioned my first artist-made house, Russel Wright's Manitoga, in 1999 with Carol Newman and the Wharton Esherick Museum in 2001.

I would also like to thank Garo Sparo, Wren Kistler, Jaime Rudolph, and Bill Lauch for their love and friendship; Janine Crowley and Blue Soho for their generous digital imaging services; Andrea Danese, my editor at Abrams, who stuck through it all; and Sarah Gifford, who designed a beautiful book.

Don Freeman

I would like to thank my friend Paul Rubé, for his encouragement and insightful editing; Phyllis Tower, for her incredible generosity of both time and knowledge at the beginning of this project; and Larry Soucy, for his friendship and support.

I would like to extend a special thanks to the librarians and staff of the Avery Architectural & Fine Arts Library, located at my alma mater, Columbia University, who collectively ensure that Avery remains the world's greatest architectural library. I particularly thank Kitty Chibnik for hunting down the inevitably elusive books and journals that I needed; Janet Parks, for locating archival materials and images; and Zachary Rose for helping to expedite book requests. Also, for their longstanding patience and assistance: Claudia Funke, Paula Gabbard, Ted Goodman, Marika Iwata, Fernela Julien-Dido, Chris Sala, Barbara Sykes-Austin, and Richard Walters.

Certain friends went out of their way to help me complete this book, notably Gordon Simpson of Anartist Books, Elizabeth Felicella, and Paul Makovsky.

Other friends generously provided shelter and transportation assistance so that I could research and visit these artist-built houses, including the Anthony family, the Rothman family, Amy Breedlove, David Anthone, Frank Futral, Dale Schafer, Phillip Schwartz, Chris Menrad, Henri Tishler and Alana Blum at Twin Gables, Michael Stone, Kara Vallow, and Jim McPherson.

Friends who provided moral support and encouragement include Brian Kish, Diana Reece, Liz O'Brien, Rob Beyer, Barry Bergdoll, James Noggle, Ferrell Mackey, Christopher London, Craig Kellogg, and Alan Rosenberg. Henry R. Kaufman provided excellent and sympathetic counsel, and Dan Sherer shared his insight, quick wit, and suggestions for this project.

I must acknowledge my immediate family, for their love and support—my parents Jerry and Sondra Gotkin, and my sister Karen Gotkin; my dear cousins for their unflagging loyalty—Kirby Kooluris, Linda Kooluris Dobbs, and our family's spiritual bulwark Myra Lanigan; and also our family's great friends, for their sustained interest and enthusiasm—Harry Sadler and Ruth Reingold Sadler.

Finally, I would also like to thank people connected with great artist-built houses not featured in the book, who nonetheless generously acted as ambassadors. In Santa Fe, Taos, and Albuquerque, New Mexico: Karyn Stockdale and Kim Straus at the Randall Davey Audubon Center & Sanctuary, Marshall Girard and family, Bill Schenck, Virgina Couse Leavitt at the The Couse Foundation, Matthew Rembe. In Woodstock, New York: Steven and Charlotte Diamond, Kristen Garnier, Clark Garnier, Laurie Ylvisaker, Renee Samuels, Josephine Bloodgood, Emily Jones, Tom Wolf, Tom Fletcher, Heather Toboika, Juma Sultan, Heidi Lennox, Ben Prosky, and Hope Prosky. In Cape Cod, Massachusetts: Mischa Richter, Julie Kepes Stone, Barbara Sass, Cliff Schorer, Todd Westrick, Chris McCarthy, Malachai Connelly, Ivan Chermayeff, Jane Clark Chermayeff, Peter Chermayeff, Andrea Peterson, Maro Chermayeff, and Sasha Chermayeff. At other locations: Kinney Freylinghausen, Kardash Onnig, John Johansen, Christen Johansen, David Daio, Charlotte Raymond, and Elli Tappan.

Michael Gotkin

PAGE 1: A detail of the tile patio at Henry Varnum Poor's Crow House.

PAGE 2: Raoul Hague studio.

PAGE 4: left: A tile at Henry Chapman Mercer's Fonthill; right: Byrdcliffe Art Colony.

PAGE 5. left: Sam Maloof's house; right: Hatch house.

PAGE 6: White Pines at Byrdcliffe Art Colony.

PAGE 7. clockwise from upper left: Russel Wright's Manitoga; Wharton Esherick's house; Sam Maloof's house; George Nakashima's house.

Editor: Andrea Danese
Designer: Sarah Gifford
Production Manager: Ankur Ghosh

Library of Congress Cataloging-in-Publication Data
Gotkin, Michael.
Artists' handmade houses / Michael Gotkin ; photography by Don Freeman.
p. cm.
ISBN 978-0-8109-9584-0 (alk. paper)
1. Artists—Homes and haunts—United States. 2. Architecture, Domestic—United States.
3. Artists' studios—United States. 4. Artists as architects—United States.
I. Freeman, Don, 1957– II. Title.
NA7195.A75G68 2010
728.0973—dc22
2010005997

House essays copyright © 2011 Michael Gotkin
Photographs copyright © 2011 Don Freeman

Published in 2011 by Abrams, an imprint of ABRAMS. All rights reserved.
No portion of this book may be reproduced, stored in a retrieval system,
or transmitted in any form or by any means, mechanical, electronic, photocopying,
recording, or otherwise, without written permission from the publisher.

Printed and bound in China

10 9 8 7 6 5 4 3 2

Abrams Books are available at special discounts when purchased in quantity
for premiums and promotions as well as fundraising or educational use.
Special editions can also be created to specification. For details, contact
specialmarkets@abramsbooks.com or the address below.

ABRAMS
THE ART OF BOOKS SINCE 1949
115 West 18th Street
New York, NY 10011
www.abramsbooks.com